D0385328

SHELTON STATE COMMUNITY
COLLEGE
JUNIOR COLLEGE DIVISION
LIBRARY

PS
3545
.098
Z55
1984

Beichman, Arnold.

Herman Wouk, the
novelist as social
historian

DATE DUE

HERMAN WOUK

DISCARDED

HERMAN WOUK

THE NOVELIST AS SOCIAL HISTORIAN

ARNOLD BEICHMAN

Transaction Books
New Brunswick (U.S.A.) and London (U.K.)

Copyright © 1984 by Transaction, Inc.
New Brunswick, New Jersey 08903

All rights reserved under International and Pan-American Copyright
Conventions. No part of this book may be reproduced or transmitted
in any form or by any means, electronic or mechanical, including
photocopy, recording, or any information storage and retrieval
system, without prior permission in writing from the publisher. All
inquiries should be addressed to Transaction Books, Rutgers—The
State University, New Brunswick, New Jersey 08903.

Library of Congress Catalog Number: 84-74

ISBN: 0-87855-498-x (cloth)

Printed in the United States of America

Library of Congress Cataloging in Publication Data

Beichman, Arnold.
  Herman Wouk, the novelist as social historian.

  Bibliography: p.
  Includes index.
  1. Wouk, Herman, 1915-   —Political and social
views. 2. Social history in literature. I. Title.
PS3545.098Z55   1984   813'.54   84-74
ISBN 0-87855-498-X

For Tony
(1939–1977)

Contents

Preface

Balzac once wrote: "I have carried an entire society in my head" (Moi, j'ai porté une société toute entière dans ma tête).[1] Few novelists today would dare make so prideful a statement nor are there any significant number of modern American novelists in whom such a talent of the imagination could be discerned. About Herman Wouk a critic might say what Balzac said about himself. The novels and plays Wouk has written in the last three decades exemplify an extraordinary, and often highly perceptive, preoccupation with American society in war and in peace.

Such a preoccupation is not as characteristic of the modern novel in America as it once was because today, as Lionel Trilling said, the novel "diverges from its classic intention, which . . . is the investigation of the problem of reality beginning in the social field. The fact is that American writers of genius have not turned their minds to society." Only Henry James in the nineteenth century knew that "to scale the moral and esthetic heights in the novel one has to use the ladder of social observation."[2]

Whatever Wouk has written, novels, plays or essays, his focus has been not merely on the inwardness of human existence and experience but also on the externals. It is as if he had taken to heart E. M. Forster's observation that "there are in the novel two forces: human beings and a bundle of various things not human beings and it is the novelist's business to conciliate their claims."[3] *Youngblood Hawke* (1962) is not only the classical *Kunstlerroman* but it is also crammed with "bundles" of detail about the New York publishing industry, Kentucky coal-mining claims, and the wild and woolly ways of Communist-hunting congressional committees in the 1950s.

It will be this writer's argument that Wouk is an unusual American novelist in that his novels are aimed at creating folkloristic tales. By this I mean stories universal in what they say to the reader, with the characters who play the tale taking on a life of their own and becoming household words. This aim, when achieved, is high novelistic art and a measure of a novelist's greatness. Such was the achievement of writers

1

like Cervantes with his Don Quixote, Proust, creator of the Baron Charlus (the old fallen prince) and, above all, Charles Dickens. And in his selection of themes, stories, and characters, Wouk speaks for the conservation of what he values best in civilization, a respect for tradition, convention, and the freedoms which comprise the efflux of democracy.

The book will deal with Wouk's eight novels, one of his three plays, and two moral tracts: his essay *This Is My God,* and the other, written as a piece of science fiction, *The "Lomokome" Papers.* The reader should keep in mind that Wouk is a rarity among Western novelists: he is an observing, practicing Orthodox Jew who spends part of each day at synagogue prayers and at home studying the *Mishna* or *Gemara,* sacred texts of Jewish ethics and faith. He spends as much time as possible in Israel, away from his home in Washington, D.C. I mention this because, as a writer, Wouk has moved counter to what has been regarded for half a century as the modern sensibility with its loss of faith, spiritual bewilderment, and the claim of man's absurdity in the eyes of his non-Creator.

One chapter will deal with what I call the politico-historical novels, the war books—*Winds of War* and *War and Remembrance*—which, because of their concern with the Henry family, might also be regarded as the *roman fleuve.* The other categories are the social novels, *Marjorie Morningstar,* a *Bildungsroman,* and *Youngblood Hawke,* referred to earlier. Then, the comic novels—*Aurora Dawn, City Boy,* and *Don't Stop the Carnival.*

The Caine Mutiny, the archetypal war novel, is regarded as one of the most influential in the World War II genre. With his Broadway play, *The Traitor,* it shares an underlying theme: Conclusive moral judgments are difficult to formulate when confronted by, on the one hand, a one-man tyranny or, on the other, intellectual hubris. The play is an amazing demonstration of art anticipating nature, prefiguring the German-Soviet physicist and atomic spy Klaus Fuchs long before he had even been publicly mentioned.[4] *The Caine Mutiny Court-Martial,* both as Broadway production and as a film, also exemplified the complexities of moral discriminations.

I had the privilege of being permitted to rummage through Wouk's papers, boxes and boxes of them, which are now on deposit, unindexed and uncollated, at Columbia University, but closed to all except for this instance. Wouk placed no restrictions on my use of the material. Working through these papers and work journals allowed me to study at close range the growth of a novelist's mind, from almost back to his days as a Fred Allen radio gag writer to his present status as a premier world novelist. (*The Caine Mutiny* alone has been translated into seventeen languages.)

For this opportunity I am grateful to Wouk and his wife, Batya Sarah, with both of whom I enjoyed several conversations during my research, and to Suzanne Stein, Wouk's literary assistant and archivist. I am also indebted to Kenneth A. Lohf, the Columbia librarian for Rare Books and Manuscripts, and his staff who made my five weeks in the manuscript reading room so pleasant.

Without the research help and thoughtful advice of my wife, Carroll Aikins Beichman, this book would not have been possible. Her reading and vetting of the manuscript was invaluable.

NOTES

1. Quoted in *The World of Modern Fiction,* ed. Steven Marcus (New York: Simon & Schuster, 1966):xvi.
2. Lionel Trilling, *The Liberal Imagination* (New York: Viking, 1950): 212–13.
3. E.M. Forster, *Aspects of the Novel* (London: Arnold, 1949): 99. As Forster says: "The novel that would express values only becomes unintelligible and therefore valueless" (p. 42).
4. Another such example of the artist's "cunning" is *The Middle of the Journey* by Lionel Trilling (New York: Viking, 1947). The novel anticipates the story of Whittaker Chambers, a central figure in one of the great espionage conspiracies of the time. In Trilling's novel, the Chambers character goes by the name of Gifford Maxim. Wouk's play was written in 1947 and produced in 1948.

Chronology

1915	Born 27 May in New York.
1921-30	Attended public schools in The Bronx, N.Y., and Townsend Harris Hall High School in Manhattan.
1934	Graduated from Columbia University with B.A. degree.
1934-36	Assistant writer for various radio comedians.
1936-41	Staff writer for comedian Fred Allen.
1941	Wrote radio scripts for U.S. Treasury's Defense Bond Campaign, as a dollar-a-year man, in Washington, D.C.
1941	Joined U.S. Navy.
1942	Graduated from midshipman school, Columbia University, and U.S. Naval Academy's communications school.
1942	Father, Abraham Isaac, died.
1943	Reported aboard U.S.S. *Zane,* a destroyer minesweeper, operating in the South Pacific.
1943	Began writing *Aurora Dawn.*
1944	Met Betty Sarah Brown, a navy personnel executive, while *Zane* was being overhauled in San Pedro, California.
1945	Assigned to U.S.S. *Southard,* another destroyer minesweeper, as executive officer, and was designated as captain, but ship struck a reef in a typhoon, and was abandoned before he took command. Discharged from navy at end of war.
1945	Married Betty Sarah Brown.
1946	Son, Abraham Isaac, born.
1947	*Aurora Dawn* published.

1948	*City Boy* published.
1948	Wrote *Slattery's Hurricane* as a screen treatment for Paramount Pictures.
1949	*The Traitor,* starring Lee Tracy and Walter Hampden, opened on Broadway.
1949	Started writing *The Caine Mutiny,* during a Naval Reserve training cruise aboard aircraft carrier *Saipan.*
1950	Son, Nathaniel, born.
1951	*The Caine Mutiny* published.
1951	Accidental death of son, Abraham Isaac, in Cuernavaca, Mexico.
1952	Awarded Pulitzer Prize for *The Caine Mutiny.*
1952-57	Visiting professor of English, Yeshiva University.
1953-54	Wrote *The Caine Mutiny Court-Martial,* which was produced on Broadway under the direction of Charles Laughton, starring Henry Fonda, Lloyd Nolan, and John Hodiak.
1954	Son, Joseph, born.
1954	Established The Abe Wouk Foundation, in memory of Abraham Isaac Wouk.
1954	Received LHD (hon.), Yeshiva University.
1955	First visit to Israel, in deputation of America-Israel Society.
1955	*Marjorie Morningstar* published.
1956	*The "Lomokome" Papers* published in *Collier's.*
1957	Grandfather, Rabbi Mendel Leib Levine, died in Israel.
1957	*Nature's Way* produced on Broadway by Alfred de Liagre, Jr.
1958	Moved to St. Thomas, V.I.
1959	*This Is My God* published.
1960	Received LLD (hon.) from Clark University.

1962	*Youngblood Hawke* published. Began research for the war books.
1962-69	Trustee, College of the Virgin Islands.
1964	Moved to Washington, D.C., to continue research in government archives.
1965	*Don't Stop the Carnival* published.
1965-75	Made several trips to do on-the-spot research in Europe, Russia, Israel, and Iran.
1971	*The Winds of War* published. Continued research, and began writing sequel.
1978	*War and Remembrance* published.
1979	DLit. (hon.) from American International College.
1979-80	Wrote television adaptation for Paramount/ABC production of *The Winds of War.*
1983	Television adaptation receives its premiere over ABC television network.

1

Early Influences

Herman Wouk, novelist, playwright, essayist, screen writer, was born on East 167th St., The Bronx, a borough of New York City, on 27 May 1915. His parents, Abraham Isaac and Esther Levine Wouk, were Russian Jews. Although they had emigrated from the same city, Minsk, in the early 1900s, they met and married in America. In Czarist Russia, Wouk's father had been a Socialist agitator under police surveillance.

His father's first job was as a three dollar a week laundry worker. Eventually he became a successful entrepreneur in the power laundry field. Like many immigrants, the family in 1931 moved from the rather depressing Bronx neighborhood to Manhattan's West End Ave., later to be one of the backgrounds of Wouk's novel *Marjorie Morningstar*.[1] (The disesteem in which this northern borough of New York City was held was expressed by a terse couplet of Ogden Nash: "The Bronx ?/ No thonx.")

Wouk was the youngest of three children, a brother, Victor, and a sister, Irene. He attended Townsend Harris High School, an elite public school for high IQ New York youngsters, later abolished in the interests of egalitarianism. At age fifteen, after a semester at Yeshiva High School, he entered Columbia College in Fall 1930 where he majored in comparative literature and philosophy.

For a teenager raised in a traditional Jewish family and with a strong grounding in the Scriptures and Talmud, Columbia was a powerful cultural influence which collided with Wouk's strongly religious background.[2] He fell away from his Orthodoxy and it was not until 1940, he has said, that he began the return, the *tshuba,* to Jewish Orthodoxy.

GRANDFATHER VERSUS PROFESSOR

Two intellectual influences were in conflict during his late teens. The first was that of his maternal grandfather, Rabbi Mendel Leib Levine,

9

who arrived from Russia in 1928 after early years of study for the rabbinate at the Volozin Yeshiva, Lithuania. The opposing influence was that of Professor Irwin Edman, Columbia's philosophy department chairman. Poet, essayist, disciple of John Dewey, and friend of George Santayana, Edman was a polished and popular lecturer and friendly to the young people around him.[3] Edman died in 1954 and Wouk's grandfather three years later in Israel.

"You might say that my career," Wouk once told a newspaper interviewer, "has been a sort of vector of these two forces—Edman and Grandpa."[4] In the same interview he described Edman as "a naturalistic skeptic of the deepest die—quite a contrast to my old Orthodox grandfather." Rabbi Levine, on the other hand, "came into my life with an assumption that the only important thing was to study the Talmud, and so great was the force of his personality that I bought the notion." In one of the folders in his Columbia archive I found some handwritten notes by Wouk which explicate perhaps a little more dramatically these influences: "The two teachers who most influenced my life were a man without a trace of Western culture and a man who is its embodiment."

This is how he describes his grandfather "who in twenty-three years of living in the United States never used the English language although he learned it." Wouk writes:

> During a lifetime stretching through ninety-four years, he did not read a novel, hear a symphony, see a play or movie, or look at a painting, classical, modern. Plato or Aristotle were shadowy names, figures more remote than Confucius or Lao-Tze are to me, a man who without question never heard of Sophocles, Dante, Cervantes, Michaelangelo, Galileo, Milton, Da Vinci, Fielding, Balzac, Dickens, Twain, or Shaw, and who, though Yiddish-speaking, never read a word of one of the world's great humorists, the equal of Molière in power and copiousness but outside of Western culture because of his Yiddish language, meaning Sholem Aleichem. This was my grandfather, Rabbi Mendel Levine, a single-minded rabbinic sage of deep wisdom and compelling charm, who cared about and taught me only one thing, the Torah.[5]

In the same folder, he described Edman whom he first encountered in a course on comparative religion, which Wouk took in his sophomore year, "but I had heard about him since the first day I had reported to Morningside Heights as a singularly crude, singularly young freshman from The Bronx."

"Edman was legendary," writes Wouk, "and looked legendary, acted legendary. He was not larger than life. Indeed, he was a good deal smaller by ordinary standards but he was more vividly colored than life. Professor Edman was little more than five feet tall. He must have been an albino. All his hair was pallid, virtually colorless, including his eyebrows and lashes, blue eyes very prominent and they oscillated back and forth all the time most disconcertingly. He was so near-sighted that when he read a book or paper, he held it practically at the end of his nose with a curious and quite characteristic sidelong glance."[6]

WOUK'S LITERARY AMBITIONS

At Columbia, Wouk's literary aspirations, already noticeable in high school and at summer camps,[7] flourished thanks to his own talents and to the help of a fellow student, Arnold Auerbach, who was a year ahead of him. (Years later, Auerbach wrote two well-known Broadway musicals, "Call Me Mister" and "Inside USA.") By graduation in June 1934, Wouk had written two varsity shows (one with Auerbach in 1933), edited the college humor magazine, the *Jester,* and had contributed a thrice-weekly humor column to the college daily, the *Columbia Spectator.*

Wouk graduated in the middle of the Depression, a period where jobs for college graduates were sparse, let alone for anyone else. Here Auerbach came to the rescue with an offer of fifteen dollars a week from David Freedman, a famous radio writer of the time. Wouk's assignment was to copy jokes out of old magazines and onto file cards and to clean up off-color gags and transmute them into radio jokes through Freedman's Formula, as it was called in "Make It with Kissing."[8] This was the title of a magazine article which Wouk wrote in 1947 when his first novel, *Aurora Dawn,* had been selected by the Book-of-the-Month Club.

Freedman's enterprise was really a joke factory for such famed radio comics as Fanny Brice, Eddie Cantor, Lou Holtz, and others. Wouk believed that the job would give him writing experience but it was rather dull work—and he began looking for something better. After two years, he found himself a niche as scriptwriter for Fred Allen. He and Auerbach each made $100 a week, a good wage in those Depression years. It was not long before they were each making $400 a week.[9]

Radio Comedy

In the magazine article Wouk defends radio comedy but in rather ironic terms, conceding that radio comedy "is a vulgar art in intention and performance . . . which, in general, is pursued with zeal, discipline, and much technical skill." He mocked the "big guns of intellectual analysis" whose attacks on radio comedy usually "end by proving triumphantly that vulgar art is vulgar." Wouk revealed a populist streak in this article by arguing that *vulgar* was a loaded word— "Franklin Roosevelt was the vulgar choice for President; it is vulgar to believe in free speech, a free press, and freedom of religion. And it is vulgar to enjoy Fred Allen, Fibber McGee, Jack Benny, and Bob Hope. That is to say, most of the people do it." Here was Wouk, sensitive so early in his as yet unborn career as a novelist, to intellectual elitism, a characteristic of "new sensibility" critics who would hound him in his later life as an outstandingly successful writer of novels, plays, films, and most recently, television drama.

Wouk defended himself and his fellow gag writers on the ground that "much serious criticism of radio seems to me that of judging one art by the standards of another. . . . Radio comedy is vaudeville. It is often judged as writing." And here Wouk became autobiographical in a far more personal sense. Referring to the "muddle of standards"—radio writing and serious writing—Wouk said, gagmen like himself were sometimes afflicted with "a sense of guilt about their profession, as though it belonged on the twilight edge of society, along with bookmaking and the selling of liquor after curfew."

During their years of gag writing, he and his collaborator, Arnold Auerbach, "devised a curious, self-deceiving fiction: We were not really gagmen, but playwrights, and what we did in radio was a sort of ditchdigging to provide food and shelter for ourselves while we pursued the high dramaturgic art." Wouk and Auerbach set themselves this ritual: Twice weekly "we would set aside an evening and talk about The Play. This served to keep alive the fantasy and refresh our spirits for a few more days of the drudgery of gag writing." Ruefully, Wouk added: "As of the moment, neither of us has written The Play."

A few years later, both of them had written successful plays. After his World War II navy experience, to which I will return later, he went back to gag writing and he tells of how he ran into an old friend, Nat Hiken, then Fred Allen's leading gag writer, at his Radio City office. Wouk describes the meeting: "Nat's tired face lit with a genial smile when he saw me. 'Ah!' said he, with genuine warmth, 'Welcome back to prostitution.' "

Popular Culture

Wouk's article is a serious examination, though written with a light touch, of American popular culture during what was the pretelevision age. For all the apologies *pro sua vita*, Wouk was already signalling his interest in how to achieve a degree of popular acceptance without compromising serious artistic standards, the problem faced by novelists from Cervantes through Richardson, Defoe, Scott, Trollope, and Dickens to the present. The Wouk article was serious in another fashion—he refused to recognize the trashy politico-cultural issue of the late 1940s about capitalist culture and its discontents, the whole argument about masscult, midcult, and high culture.

Wouk said that radio humor was a way of solving a particular problem: "Given an invention which enables millions of people to enjoy a vaudeville act all at once, instead of a few hundred at a time over a period of years, how shall the amusement be maintained week in, week out? The solution is to keep the form of the vaudeville act but renew its substance each week." To illustrate the point, Wouk used a sprightly metaphor. Radio is a sort of "doughnut machine of vaudeville, using fresh ingredients in each operation but always producing the same kind of doughnut. The renewable ingredients of comic vaudeville are jokes."

The period during which Wouk worked as a radio humorist (according to him there were never more than about 200 gag writers at any one time) was the golden age of famous radio comedy stars, an era not likely to be duplicated in the television era, whether commercial or cable—comics like Ed Wynn, Jack Pearl, Bert Lahr, Burns and Allen, Milton Berle, Henry Youngman, Abbott and Costello, Jack Benny, and, of course, Fred Allen.

Farewell to Radio

In the article Wouk felt it necessary to explain why he was saying farewell, after thirteen financially rewarding years, to "gag writing as a useful and rewarding trade." (At the end of that career, he was earning about $500 a week in those memorable preinflation dollars.) Although the pay was good, if uncertain, "the life of the gagman, with its tension, its long, irregular hours . . . its color and excitement, is really bachelors' work—young bachelors preferably—and I, a family man entering the sere and yellow thirties, was already feeling, at some postwar gag conference, a little like the Last Leaf."[10] And there was also the desire "of wanting to see my work in print, and the career of refueling vaudeville acts is one of perpetual anonymity."

THE WAR YEARS

In 1941, the Auerbach-Wouk partnership broke up as the war neared American shores. In June of that year he went to Washington as a dollar-a-year man to write radio scripts for the war-bond selling campaign of the U.S. Treasury. He had earlier attempted to join the navy but was unable to get into officers' training school because an engineering background was a prerequisite. With Pearl Harbor, the standards for entry were lowered and he entered midshipman's school at Columbia University, a different kind of "return."[11]

He graduated from midshipmen's school in the top twenty of a class of 500. By now he had returned to Orthodox Judaism and throughout his four years in the navy, he held to Jewish laws and customs, particularly about *kashruth*, i.e., food prepared in accordance with Jewish dietary laws. On the *Liberty* ship which took him to the Pacific in 1942, Wouk often ate nothing but bread and potatoes, because the ship's menu emphasized pork almost exclusively. One day he posted a poem on the bulletin board:

> *Of all God's creatures small and big*
> *We owe most to our friend, the pig. . .*
> *Yeoman, record this in the log:*
> *Twenty-one-gun salute—the hog!*

A senior officer saw the "four-liner," found out who had written it, and issued an order to the kitchen: "Give this man something he can eat."[12]

In the Wouk archive, I found a handwritten entry dated 11 April 1965 describing a White House dinner given by President Lyndon B. Johnson in honor of the president of Upper Volta and to which Wouk and his wife had been invited:[13] "We couldn't eat anything at the White House naturally except some vegetables. As I recall there was a seafood dish and then some roast beef which looked very good. The dessert was an ice-cream thing which we did eat. Several wines went with this and I had to hold back to avoid getting looped."[14]

For Wouk, the wartime navy was "the great experience of my life." In the navy, he said, "I found out more than I ever had about people and the United States. I had always been a word boy, and suddenly I had to cope with the peculiar, marvelous world of the machine."[15]

In February 1943 he was assigned to a World War I four-piper refitted as a destroyer-minesweeper, the U.S.S. *Zane,* at anchor in the South Pacific in a harbor near Guadalcanal. From assistant communications officer he moved up steadily in rank to become the ship's first lieutenant and navigator. The *Zane* swept mines off the Marshalls, Kwajalein, Eniwetok, the Marianas, Guam, Saipan, Tinian. Later he was assigned to another minesweeper, the U.S.S. *Southard*, and there was more action. In all, Wouk took part in eight Pacific invasions, won four campaign stars and a unit citation. When the war ended, he had become the ship's executive officer and had been recommended to relieve the captain of the *Southard*, but the ship was wrecked during a typhoon off Okinawa in October 1945 and was abandoned before he could take command.

HOW IT BEGAN

On a somewhat earlier occasion, the *Zane* needed to undergo repairs, but this time it was at the navy yard in San Pedro, California. It was in late 1944 when Wouk and some fellow officers disembarked for a night on the town, which might have ended when the bars closed except that one of the officers remembered a birthday party being given for the boss of a file clerk he knew. *Time* quotes Wouk: "So we all barged in. I made a date with one of the file clerks for lunch the next day. All through lunch the girl raved about her boss, this beautiful, witty, talented creature. Naturally I went back to her office to take a second look, and I made a date with the boss."

The "boss" was Betty Brown, a red-headed Phi Beta Kappa from the University of Southern California and then a navy personnel executive. Betty was a Protestant but not a practicing one. Both fell in love. When Wouk returned to his ship, Betty Brown began the study of Judaism and a year later, on her twenty-fifth birthday, she became a Jewish convert.

On 1 December 1945, Wouk was demobilized. He was just about thirty years old. Nine days after his demobilization and arrival in California he married Betty Brown. She took the Hebrew name— Sarah Batya, which means "daughter of God" in Hebrew. And then to work—finishing the novel begun at sea, *Aurora Dawn*.

The Early Novels

Wouk apparently did a lot of writing while at sea. The habit of writing in longhand was acquired during his navy life because most of his writing occurred at hours when others slept—an hour or two each day before dawn—and a typewriter would have been an imposition on the crew.

The idea for his first novel, *Aurora Dawn*, came to him while he was on the U.S.S. *Zane*. According to Wouk, the ship had crashed on a reef and had to put into Auckland, New Zealand, for repairs to the ship's propeller. With nothing much to do except wait for the repairs, Wouk went into an Auckland bookstore where there was nothing on the book shelves but eighteenth- and ninteenth-century novels. He bought up the lot and, as he said, "I read everything I thought I was going to read sometime."[16] There he had discovered Cervantes, whose *Don Quixote*, said Wouk, is "the key to my entire career. I read it for the first time at twenty-nine and that was when I decided I should try to write novels."[17] It was Cervantes's narrative power which inspired him, he told me. By now he was "impregnated" with eighteenth- and ninteenth-century writers who, in Wouk's phrase, "had a commitment to entertainment."

At sea, Wouk had finished four chapters of *Aurora Dawn* and a synopsis which he then sent off to Professor Edman at Columbia University. A few days later, Edman took the chapters with him to lunch with Henry Simon, brother of Richard Simon of Simon & Schuster. He quoted—"Edman had an almost photographic memory," Wouk told me—from the chapters to Simon and left the manuscript and synopsis with the publishers.

It was while in Okinawa, where the *Southard* had cracked up during a storm, and with it Wouk's chance to be a ship's captain, that he got the news—Simon & Schuster would publish the novel on completion. Back on land, he finished the manuscript in May 1946 and formally dedicated it, on publication, to Edman. The book became a May 1947 selection of the Book-of-the-Month Club, a rather striking achievement for a first-time novelist.

His next novel was based on his Bronx boyhood—*City Boy*, the growing up of an eleven-year-old, which was published in 1948. It had a slow start with new editions appearing in 1952 and 1969. Twenty-five years after publication, in 1973, it was made an alternate selection of the Book-of-the-Month Club. The book is now widely used in English elementary courses as the story of The Bronx's Tom Sawyer.

The Caine Mutiny was published in March 1951 and suffered a slow start; no major book club had chosen it. There was no rush by readers to bookstores. Yet somehow word got around. There was a second printing in April and four printings the following June. By September *The Caine Mutiny* had replaced James Jones's *From Here to Eternity* as the country's number one best-seller. The novel led the best-seller list for a year. In May 1952, it won the Pulitzer Prize for fiction. Only then did the book clubs adopt it as their alternate selection, while more than half a million copies of the novel had been sold in bookstores. It has sold far more than three million copies, been published in seventeen foreign languages, and became a successful play and, later, a motion picture with Humphrey Bogart as the tragic Captain Queeg. The play was based on the novel's court sequence and was called *The Caine Mutiny Court-Martial*. It was, of course, written by Wouk.

His next novel was highly controversial: *Marjorie Morningstar,* a New York Jewish girl, starry-eyed, ambitious, craving popularity, suitors, theater stardom. Despite the conventional wisdom that novels on Jewish themes could not be successful, Wouk's 1955 novel became a best-seller and, like all his subsequent novels, a major book club selection.

While writing his next novel, *Youngblood Hawke,* he interrupted his work to execute an idea he had been thinking about for some years, in his own words, "a fairly short and clear account of the Jewish faith from a personal viewpoint." He called it *This Is My God,* and dedicated it to the memory of his grandfather. The book was on the best-seller lists for half a year and is regarded as a standard work on Judaism. The copyright of this book was donated by Wouk and his wife to the Abe Wouk Foundation, named in memory of their first-born son who died accidentally at the age of five.

Youngblood Hawke, published in 1962, gave a detailed, Balzacian view of the New York and Hollywood literary life, in part reflecting, like many of Wouk's novels, the author's personal experiences, although the novel is in no sense autobiographical.[18]

The War Novels

On publication day of *Youngblood Hawke,* 17 May 1962, Wouk began to outline his novel *The Winds of War,* a tale that would, as Wouk expressed it "in a phrase Joseph Conrad used about a Napoleonic novel he never wrote—'throw a rope around' the Hitler era." By then he was living in the Virgin Islands with his wife and two young sons. Interspersed with his war novel research was the concurrent writing of a short tragicomic novel, *Don't Stop the Carnival,* a narrative about life and death on a mythical Caribbean island. It was published in 1965.

In 1964, the Wouks settled in Washington, D.C., where it was easier to carry on the research for the war novels, particularly interviewing surviving military leaders and enjoying access to the National Archives and the Library of Congress. They purchased and renovated in the Georgetown section of Washington an 1815 house to be used as a combined office and residence. *Winds of War* was published in 1971 and ten years later, Wouk's television adaptation of the novel for the ABC/Paramount production was ready for showing. Work on the second volume of the World War II epic continued and was published in 1978 under the title *War and Remembrance.*[19]

Interspersed with the novels were plays and short stories, and one novelette, a science fiction tale, *The "Lomokome" Papers.* A play,

Nature's Way, was produced on Broadway in 1957. There are a number of short stories, published and unpublished, among five boxes in the Wouk archive.[20]

THE WOUK FAMILY

The Wouks live a fairly retired life, alternating between their Georgetown home, a retreat in Middleburg, Virginia, and frequent long stays in Israel. The author's avocation is Judaic scholarship, as it is also that of his now grown sons, the elder, Nathaniel, a Princeton graduate, embarked on a career as a novelist, and Joseph, a Columbia Law School graduate, who has become an Israeli citizen and has entered the Israeli Department of Justice.

There is one particular note worth making: the tremendous importance that Mrs. Wouk plays in the final preparation of her husband's manuscripts. In one of the boxes of the Wouk archive, I found this note concerning *Winds of War:* "I have read aloud this work, like all my other works, chapter by chapter to my wife. She has done two careful editorial readings. She is a brilliant, self-effacing woman, whose critical and creative suggestions are imbedded in all my books and plays beyond disentanglement."[21]

NOTES

1. For a historical discussion of these various Jewish migrations see Deborah Dash Moore, *At Home In America: Second Generation New York Jews* (New York: Columbia University Press, 1981).
2. "You, Me, and the Novel," *Saturday Review* (29 June 1974): 13.
3. For a taste of Edman's charming urbanity and wit, see his collection of essays *Philosopher's Holiday.* Reprinted as *Philosopher's Quest,* Greenberg Publishers, 1973.
4. Irwin Ross, *New York Post* (17 January 1956): 39. This was one of a six-part series on Wouk which ran in the New York daily during 16-21 January 1956, at about the time *Marjorie Morningstar* was published. Wouk was later critical of most of the quotes in the articles. *New York Post* (23 January 1956).
5. Although Wouk does not discuss the reasons for his grandfather's disregard of Western culture, they were not antiintellectual but religious in origin. Painting and sculpture for a strongly Orthodox Jew could be explained as violating the second commandment: "Thou shalt not make unto thee any graven image." The father of Isaac Bashevis Singer could have been described in essentially the same way as Wouk's grandfather. See Singer, *In My Father's Court* (New York: Farrar, Straus, & Giroux, 1966): 51, 68, 171, passim. Also Edward Alexander, *Isaac Bashevis Singer* (Boston: Twayne, 1980), ch. 1.

6. Since the Wouk archive at Columbia is neither indexed nor collated nor is there any likelihood that it will be in the near future, and since it is still accumulating—there are fifty-odd volumes of work journals of which I have only seen a fraction; not all of them are at Columbia—there is no way properly to footnote my citations, except for the generic category "Wouk Papers." Regarding Wouk's description of Edman, I can vouch for its accuracy and detail since, as a classmate of Wouk's and campus (but not personal) friend, I took the same course in comparative religion.

7. According to the *New York Post* (17 January 1956), Wouk was writing poetry at the age of eight or nine and was fascinated by dramatics. His sister described him as a superb storyteller. His mother recalled that he was an omnivorous reader and when there was nothing to read he liked to curl up near the radiator with a dictionary. He also had a passion for science fiction magazines.

8. Herman Wouk, "Make It with Kissing," *'47* (November 1947): 14. The name of the magazine, now defunct, was to change with the calendar year. It was edited by Clifton Fadiman, the eminent literary critic, during its short span. Much of what follows about Wouk's years as a gag writer is a summary of the article, which was subtitled "An Unrepentant Gag-Writer's Farewell to Radio Humor."

9. The work of a gag writer consisted of turning out some sixty pages of dialogue every week for thirty-nine weeks of the radio season plus a humorous version of "investigative journalism"—reports on the bagel industry, interviews with a worm salesman, a goldfish doctor, and the man who put the cloves in the hams in the window of a famed Broadway restaurant. Of all radio comics in the pre–World War II period, Fred Allen was the most highly regarded along with Henry Morgan, for whom Wouk also did some writing.

10. Wouk has a penchant for classical references, noticeable in this article. The "sere and yellow" phrase is from Macbeth's speech (Act V, Sc. 3); the "Last Leaf" is a variant of the line from Tennyson's *In Memoriam:* "The last red leaf is whirl'd away. . . ." In other parts of the article he refers to "bare ruined choirs, where late the sweet birds sang," from Shakespeare's seventy-third sonnet. Gag writers "summon wheezes from the vasty deep," a Wouk improvisation on a line from *Henry IV* (Part I, Sc. 3).

11. "Herman Wouk," *Publisher's Weekly* (7 February 1972): 44. He also attended during this period communications school at Annapolis.

12. "The Wouk Mutiny," *Time* cover story (5 September 1955): 50. Subsequent quotes are from *Time* unless otherwise indicated.

13. "Wouk papers." In Fall 1981, the Wouks were dinner guests at a White House function for Prime Minister Menachem Begin. One can assume that in these circumstances the food, in deference to Mr. Begin, was kosher.

14. In 1955, Wouk and his wife were visiting David Ben-Gurion in his retreat in the Negev. As Wouk later told the story of his conversation with the Israeli prime minister: "Toward the end of our visit, Ben-Gurion said he would like to have us stay for dinner, but he couldn't. You see"—with a chuckle—"he doesn't keep a kosher home." *New York Post* (19 January 1956): 4.

15. His "love affair" with the navy continued even after the war. As a reserve officer in 1949, he boarded the U.S.S. *Saipan,* an aircraft carrier, at about

the same time he began writing *The Caine Mutiny*. In 1967, he spent three weeks on the U.S.S. *Sirago,* a fleet submarine cruising around the Caribbean around the Virgin Islands, and engaged in torpedo attack and evasion exercises. "I could have stayed aboard the submarine with pleasure," he wrote in his journals. "Wouk papers." The quote in the text is from the *New York Post* (17 January 1956).

16. I interviewed Wouk on 7 August 1980 at a rented summer home in Malibu Beach, California. I will, of course, discuss *Aurora Dawn* in chapter 2, in greater detail.

17. *Book World* (26 December 1971): 14.

18. Wouk spent some time in Hollywood writing the screen treatment for a 20th Century-Fox film, *Slattery's Hurricane*. While researching *The Caine Mutiny,* he came across a story idea about hurricane-hunting airplane pilots, turned it into a magazine article first and then a screenplay. The film, shown in 1949, included as the leading players Richard Widmark, Linda Darnell, and Veronica Lake.

19. According to his work journals, Wouk wrote the first words of *Winds of War* in July 1965 and the last words of *War and Remembrance* in July 1978—thirteen years of research, reading, and writing.

20. One of the boxes in the Wouk archive contains four drafts of *The "Lomokome" Papers*. The unpublished stories—*Slattery's Hurricane* was published in the July 1949 issue of the defunct *American Magazine* as a short novel—include "The Queerest Business" (1947) and "The Great Linda" (1951), both dealing with the theater; "Absolute Power Corrupts Absolutely" (1951), "Murder of Quayle," and "The Irresistible Force," undated. The July 1949 *Cosmopolitan* published a short story called "Red Head," the original Wouk title, "The Esthetic Evening of Tom Colwell." One short story, "The Star," became the basis of a Wouk memorandum to himself: "This is abominable. I wrote it on a typewriter in three hours. The answer seems to be that I cannot write well with a pace of 1,000 words an hour. There is no structure, no surprise, no interest. It is dead and flat as a college theme. It has no humor and except in a line or two at the end, no apparent understanding of people. . . . It amazes me that I could write such a piece. It shows retrogression of fifteen years. I can see now how reputable authors produce garbage. It does happen. At least I have the sense not to show this anywhere as my handwork." The memo is dated 22 July 1947.

21. In one folder of the archive, titled "Work in Progress," I found a 27-page, single-spaced, page-by-page critique by Mrs. Wouk of *Winds of War*. A perusal of the manuscript would indicate that Wouk's wife is a severe and highly intelligent critic.

2

A Good Start: *Aurora Dawn*

Before it became a novel, *Aurora Dawn* was a play. Perhaps because it seemed to Wouk that playwriting was easy and novel writing supremely difficult he opted for the stage. After all, at Columbia College he had in 1933 coauthored a varsity show, "Home, James," and in 1934, on his own, "Laugh it Off." Dialogue came naturally to someone who had spent six successful and profitable years writing radio vaudeville comedy. He had worked on a play titled "Meadow Sweet with Hay," based on the poetic idyl by John Greenleaf Whittier. As he thought of it, writing a play was nothing more than five Fred Allen sketches. The illusion was finally dispelled after an inauspicious beginning.

While he was on the U.S.S. *Zane* charging around the Pacific, he began a play on 12 July 1943, according to his work journal, a satire on Madison Avenue radio advertising and by implication on the business mentality which, says Wouk's note to himself, "I conceive to be the chief folly of our time." There was no explanation as to the meaning of "chief folly," but the intention to satirize the commercial radio business was foremost in Wouk's mind as he began the play.

Three months later, 15 October 1943, having written one and a half acts, he wrote in his journal: "I have a sudden irresistible impulse to try to make a novel out of the material of *Aurora Dawn*." During a refitting in New Zealand of his damaged navy vessel, he had immersed himself in eighteenth- and nineteenth-century English novels and *Don Quixote*—all that there was in the local Auckland bookstore—and then thought of a switch to the novel form. As he wrote in his journal:

21

My first effort to contain it [*Aurora Dawn*] in a play is a failure. Since I last did work on it, I've been thinking and thinking about its failure and trying to piece out a better pattern for it. At the same time I've read a couple of novels with heroes, to wit—*Joseph Andrews, Nicholas Nickelby*—and I am now engrossed in *Don Quixote.* The form of those narratives, the looseness, the irony, the authors' interpellations, the fundamental optimism, the scorn for affectation, all these have meant a great deal for me. I despise the solemnity of modern hacks. Would it be possible to write a story in the wonderful tradition of Fielding, Cervantes, Smollett, Thackeray, and Dickens admitting at the outset that I had not the maturity nor the wit nor the inventiveness for the job. . . .

I know this may be a device I'm using to dodge out of the obligation of writing *Aurora Dawn* which somehow I can no longer feel as a play. Well, even if I scrawl a few pages of pastiche Fielding-Dickens and then quit ignominiously I must let the demon be exorcised. I am right to remain in possession at least. For the moment I will be riding the crest of the creative impulse again. At best I may actually draft out an amusing novel.

THE PLAY'S NOT *THE THING*

What had started Wouk thinking of shifting from play to novel was his realization as he reread the one and a half acts that, as he told me, "the stage directions were better than the dialogue." He had realized that the "narrative power" of Cervantes was a reason for the greatness of *Don Quixote* and Wouk said he thought that there was the beginning of a similar narrative power in the stage directions. So—the play's not the thing; the classical novel is.[1]

Aurora Dawn can be described as an old-fashioned moral tale about a bright, amiable young man, Andrew Reale, born in Colorado, educated at Yale, and now a minor executive in the advertising sales department of one of the two major U.S. broadcasting networks. He is in love with a beautiful, virginal photographer's model, Laura Beaton, known as Honey, who is in love with Andrew. The time is the pretelevision 1930s, the year 1937.

Much attracted to Honey, the glamorous model, is Stephen English, a fortyish bank millionaire with little to do now that he has divorced his childless wife. He is a patron of the arts and sciences. English has a painter friend, Michael Wilde, referred to ironically as "Bezalel" because he inserted in his illustrated edition of the Bible a full-length portrait of himself in Old Testament dress, as a representation of the divinely inspired artist who built the Tabernacle.[2] Wilde, at English's direction, is to paint Honey for some charity booklet during a community chest drive.

A Boorish Corporate Tycoon

Talmadge Marquis, president of a company which sponsors many radio programs and is, therefore, feared in the industry, supervises the rehearsals and performances of his many radio shows.[3] His supervision is in no way handicapped by his egregious taste and ignorance of what passes for entertainment values in the industry. His daughter Carol, a shrewd eighteen-year-old described by the author as the "beautiful Brahmin" (for want of a real name as the novel opens), is on a train heading for Washington, D.C. when she runs into Andrew Reale on the same train. Reale is heading down to the hills of West Virginia to meet a lay preacher, Father Calvin Stanfield, whose nationally broadcast sermons have given him a wide religious following.

Reale successfully persuades Father Stanfield to go on a nationwide radio program for a pink soap called, redundantly, Aurora Dawn. In the faraway and long ago days when the Marquis Company was founded the soap had been named Aurora. The soap wrapper showed a nude, rosy maiden emerging from a sunrise. The mythical allusion was regarded as too obscure and so "(dawn)" was inserted under "Aurora." A few years later, the company's board of directors took a courageous step. Since housewives called it the "Aurora Dawn" soap, the directors dropped the parentheses and thus bowed to popular will.

Antiadvertising Speech

Although Reale is engaged to be married to Honey, he is tempted by Carol Marquis as the means whereby he could obtain control of the Marquis enterprise. Reale breaks his engagement with Honey and proposes to Carol. The scheme all comes to naught because of the following sequence of events:

At a dinner party in honor of Father Stanfield at the Marquis home, Michael Wilde, the maverick painter, in an after-dinner monologue delivers a witty denunciation of radio advertising (it is not clear why newspaper or magazine advertising is exempt) designed to make Reale ridiculous in the eyes of Carol Marquis. Father Stanfield adapts this monologue as the subject matter for his next radio sermon.

The corporate dictator, Marquis, reads the script of the Stanfield sermon before delivery and refuses to let the program be broadcast in that form. Encouraged by the mischievous Wilde, the preacher distributed the controversial script to the press and with it a protest against suppression of religious freedom by the power of gold.

There is a nationwide protest against the Marquis action and a threatened boycott of Aurora Dawn and all other company products.

But Marquis refuses to back down and the broadcasting company is frightened by talk of a federal investigation. Andrew Reale sides with Marquis, largely to further his suit with Carol. He attempts to persuade his superiors in the network to exclude Stanfield from the studios. As a result, he loses his position with the network and Stanfield makes his broadcast. That same night, the jilted Laura or Honey Beaton marries Stephen English. As they leave the scene of their church wedding, they are injured in an auto accident and hospitalized.

Mrs. Smollett, Dea Ex Machina

Public opinion, however, is still outraged and remains unappeased by the Rev. Stanfield's victory over the forces of corporate greed. So the company's board of directors sets a meeting where Marquis's resignation will be demanded. At this point, an English lady, Gracie Smollett, runs into Reale at the broadcasting studios. She is looking for Stanfield. Reale introduces himself as the Reverend's secretary and takes her out for a drink. He learns that Mrs. Smollett had been, twenty years earlier during Stanfield's World War I soldiering, the Reverend's paramour for three weeks in England and that, unbeknownst to him, she had borne him a son.

Andrew determines to use this knowledge to force from this *chevalier sans peur et sans reproche* a signed statement to be used in absolving Marquis and praising his religious qualities. Apparently Stanfield's fear of exposure forces him to comply. However, there is no real clue as to either internal or external causation for Stanfield's signing a statement which, says the preacher to Reale, "is the first lie I've told since I was younger'n you."

Reale returns to his office prepared to receive the gift for his piece of blackmail, the hand of Carol Marquis. On his desk he finds a letter from Carol saying she is eloping with Wilde, the artist, whose condemnation of her father and of radio advertising inspired Stanfield and initiated the crisis. Overcome by what he has done and what has happened, Reale runs after the messenger to whom he had entrusted the precious Stanfield confession for delivery to Marquis. The confession would have been presented to the Board of Directors meeting as Marquis's vindication. On the steps of Marquis's home, he grabs the messenger and takes back the Stanfield confession. In an instant, as a purificatory act, he tears it to pieces, destroys his hopes of making a fortune as a Marquis subordinate, and runs through the streets shouting, "Free! Free!" Marquis manages to save himself without the confession and eventually recaptures his old authority.[4]

The auto accident after the Honey Beaton-English marriage leads to its dissolution at the prompting of the badly injured husband who realizes that his wife is still in love with Reale, the penitent. The happy couple go off to a ranch, which Honey has inherited, and Reale realizes the folly of his worldly ambitions at the unusually early age of twenty-six. And Aurora Dawn, of course, stays in business, and business is good.

WHAT A FIRST NOVEL TELLS

For his first novel—and there is no doubt that Wouk had determined to be a writer—he chose to weave his plot around a subject he knew a great deal about, radio advertising. It was an intelligent selection because it immediately eliminated the need for the elaborate and meticulous research which characterizes his later novels, particularly the books about World War II. In a sense he had no alternative but to write a novel (or a play) about radio advertising because there was no way he could research anything out there in the Pacific on a destroyer-minesweeper or, later, on Okinawa. Of course, when he returned to the U.S. and was mustered out of the navy, he could then research, but having worked on the novel until 1945 and then having sold it to Simon & Schuster, there was no turning back.[5]

The first work of any novelist tells us much about him and his future course as an artist. Anthony Powell's first novel, *Afternoon Men* (1931), was "a comic masterpiece," as Bernard Bergonzi wrote.[6] Evelyn Waugh's *Decline and Fall* (1928), Norman Mailer's *The Naked and the Dead* (1948), like Powell's, were first novels that told readers they had something to look forward to. While some novelists never recover from a successful first novel, others get better and surer in their artistry and narrative skill with each new work.

Aurora Dawn was a finger exercise by a budding novelist who was in the process of learning how to synthesize experience into plausible narrative, decorated with satirical flair and broadly drawn characters living in a world of hard dollars and pliable morality. It also showed a writer who was widely read, particularly in the classics and the Bible, in philosophy and psychology, one who dealt genially with the personalities in his novel and who openly and consciously was determined to avoid salaciousness or vulgarity.[7] He is hostile to the dominant Freudianism of the period and to what he calls the "conventional" rules of literary creativity. To be hostile to Freudian doctrine at the time Wouk was beginning to be published was to run counter to High Culture in Eastern universities and to the powerful literary critics of New York intellectualdom.[8]

Athough Wouk tries, in keeping with the Richardson-Fielding canon he seeks to emulate in *Aurora Dawn,* to avoid moral indignation, it is quite clear from the many asides that he has strong feelings about what was becoming permissible in the postwar 1940s in the novel: first, sex as a novel's subject matter, and second, the use to which psychology is put to support this permissiveness. For example, talking about the happy marriage of Honey Beaton's parents, Wouk writes:

> . . . indeed, they loved each other, and were innocent enough to be completely, unreflectively pleased with this love, not having any other experience with which to compare it and not being aware of the explicit standards set forth in modern treatises on the mechanics of connubial bliss, or the transcendent ecstasies hinted at in French novels. They grew old together in the unconscious contentment which the loose nomenclature of former days called happiness.[9]

Wouk is also raising the flag of moral behavior basing himself on a secularist philosopher rather than on any of the sacred revelations and teachings of ancient Judaism.[10] He cites Immanuel Kant's "important distinction between *arbitrium sensitivum* and *arbitrium brutum* in his inquiry into the possibility of free will and moral responsibility," or the age-old question between free will and determinism. Wouk writes: "Morality is eternal; but its modes fluctuate." He makes the point that the manners of the time and place change and society in the 1930s "took an exceedingly frivolous view of the importance of holding hands, and indeed of other, somewhat more searching liberties."[11] Later he distinguishes between moral and historical truth (p. 128).

WOUK'S LITERARY HERITAGE

There are a number of other points to be made about *Aurora Dawn.* First, for a Jewish author who often alludes, as indicated earlier, to the Old Testament and Judaism generally, it is surprising that not a single character in the novel is Jewish even though the main scenes are in New York City. (It could be, of course, that in the year in which the novel's action occurs, 1937, there were no leading executives in radio advertising or in the radio networks who were Jewish.) Second, he is quite self-conscious of his frequent allusions to philosophers and classical authors. In the eighteenth-century English novelistic style he has adopted here, he explains why:

> Cervantes, in his preface to the book of books (this side of Holy Writ, of course), heaps red coals of satire on pedantry. . . . Lest anyone think I have neither read nor taken to heart that lesson, I say here . . . that I do

not expect the kindest critic to mistake such scraps of learning for scholarship. Every author is entitled to take his hobby-horse for a brief canter now and then; mine is a partiality toward the ancients.[12]

Third, the effect of his reading of the classic novelists had been momentous for a beginner. Wouk found himself early with *Aurora Dawn*. He had repudiated the modern novel, its protagonists and the stream of consciousness technique whereby a novel's central characters

> may and generally do commit all the grosser sins in the arsenal of wickedness . . . the events are so obscured by the heroes' protracted maundering to themselves, usually rendered by the artistic machinery of broken phrases, bad grammar, and no punctuation, that the reader comes to sympathize with the rascals, or at least to overlook their garish misdeeds. Poor Andy, however, is never permitted to drivel in this way; his faults are set forth in straightforward storytelling, and by his acts you must judge him.[13]

Fourth, it is also clear that Wouk's religious faith will play a dominant role in his novels. Andrew Reale's attendance at the Fifth Ave. church where the jilted Honey Beaton is marrying the aging Stephen English (p. 170) is described by Wouk ironically, even ungenerously. Andrew feels out of place in the church:

> Churches to him were natural facts of existence, like fire plugs; they were to be seen in civilized communities, and surely were of use, but warranted no narrow inquiry into their origins. . . . He had not prayed since he had prayed in vain at the age of twelve that his father might not die, and he had not been inside a church, save for weddings, in ten years. He was, in short, a thoroughly modern and enlightened young man.[14]

Wouks' Andrew Reale character is influenced by *Joseph Andrews* and *Gil Blas,* the four-volume novel of Alain-René Lesage, which appeared seriatim between 1715 and 1735.[15] The hero in each of the three works is an ordinary young man who becomes the victim of "robbers" (and, surely, from Wouk's feelings about the radio advertising business or at least as the artist-intellectual Wilde expresses it, the word *robbers* is not misapplied). However, they learn from their experiences; and Gil Blas, a corrupted cleric who learns wisdom from his experiences in jail, and Joseph Andrews, are clearly Andrew Reale's prototypes.

One last point is probably the most important and is challengingly composed by Wouk himself in the last chapter and in the epilogue. The challenge encompasses Wouk's theory of the novel, that it must first be entertaining in the Dickens-Fielding-Richardson-Cervantes tradition or as the title of the epilogue puts it, "in which the author takes discreet cognizance of the maxim, 'The tale may have a moral, but plain folks follow the story.' "

Wouk begins the last chapter with this sentence: "Every novel nowadays is supposed to have a purpose, not the purpose of instructive entertainment which was the sole aim of literature for several thousand years until it suddenly obsolesced a few decades ago, but the purpose of correcting a specific social disorder such as capitalism, deforestation, inadequate city planning, war or (as some authors view it) religion." This obsolescence began with Emile Zola who discovered, says Wouk, "at the start of the century that 'Truth is on the march.' It is evidently still marching . . . and so it behooves literature to get into step and move to the regulated candence of Purpose."[16]

If any reader thought the moral of the story—Wouk is at pains to call it a moral, not a "literary message"—is that modeling is a terrible profession for young ladies or that radio and advertising are "the curse of our age," he has misread the novel. The moral of the story "is only the Pardoner's Latin platitude, threadbare half a thousand years ago or to revert to the plain English of the first sentence of this book, 'The road to happiness does not necessarily lie in becoming rich very quickly.' "[17]

This last instance of story development—the unexpected switch—characterizes some of Wouk's later novels, notably *The Caine Mutiny*. It is also a reason for the attacks on Wouk by some literary and academic intellectuals who have camouflaged political biases with the colors of literary theory.

NOTES

1. After the warm reception of the novel and at the suggestion of Kurt Weill, the German-American composer, Wouk went to work on the novel as a possible musical comedy. He had just about finished the job when he picked up the paper one morning to read that Weill had suddenly died. They had had eight work sessions during the summer of 1947 and then suspended the talks because Weill was heavily committed to the production of "Lost in the Stars," a musical based on Alan Paton's *Cry the Beloved Country*.
2. Exodus, xxxi, 1-6. The name, in Hebrew, means "in the shadow of God."
3. Marquis, the businessman-villain, may well have been inspired by Wouk's having read earlier while aboard his naval vessel *Nicholas Nickelby*. Ralph Nickelby, Nicholas's egregious uncle, was a miserly usurer whom Dickens describes in this fashion: "He knew himself well, and choosing to imagine that all mankind were cast in the same mould, hated them." There might

even be a touch of Nicholas Nickelby in Andrew Reale. Just as Nicholas had renounced the inheritance from a remorseful Uncle Ralph who hung himself for a misdeed, so Reale walks out on the radio advertising business at the moment of his greatest success. There is another touch of Nickelby in this novel. The instant cause of Uncle Ralph's suicide is his discovery that a half-witted drudge, Smike, whom Nicholas befriended but whom Uncle Ralph persecuted until he died, was Uncle Ralph's son by a secret marriage. In Wouk's novel, there was long ago an inamorata of Father Stanfield out of which had come, unknown to the radio preacher, a son now grown.

4. In Wouk's summary of the novel, which is dedicated to Professor Edman and prepared before he had completed it, the Stanfield confession is not torn up by Reale. Marquis gets it and with its presentation to the Board of Directors, Marquis triumphs and carries the day. The original summary, which presumably was presented to Simon & Schuster, gave the novel's subtitle, "A Wholesome Novel" and had as its byline, Herman Z. Wouk. The "Z" has never been used in print. The subtitle of the published novel reads: *or, The True History of Andrew Reale Containing a Faithful Account of the Great Riot, Together with the Complete Texts of Michael Wilde's Oration and Father Stanfield's Sermon.* The original edition being out of print, a new edition was published in 1956, following publication of *The Caine Mutiny* and *Marjorie Morningstar.* The new reprint had drawings by a popular caricaturist and cartoonist of the period, Alajálov. The publishers of the reissue were Doubleday, which had just published *Marjorie Morningstar.*

5. Publication of *Aurora Dawn* coincided with the publication of *The Hucksters* by Frederic Wakeman, something which the reviewers of Wouk's book commented on at the time. There is little question that the somewhat earlier novel had an influence on Wouk, who in an introduction to the novel refers to the "points of similarity" between his novel and others "intended to expose the inner workings of the advertising industry." Advertising and advertising agencies have been a favorite target of American writers. Raymond Chandler once said: "Chess is as elaborate a waste of human intelligence as you could find anywhere outside an advertising agency." There were some changes between his presentation of the summary to Simon & Schuster and the final manuscript as indicated in note 4. Another change is in the name of the business tycoon, originally Thomas Jefferson Marquis but in the final manuscript changed to Talmadge, a rather unusual first name but more meaningful since it was the surname of an unpopular Southern politician of the time. Onomastics are most important to Wouk as one will note later in the names of many of his characters.

6. Bernard Bergonzi, *Anthony Powell* (London: Longman, 1962):3.

7. Pagination in these notes follows the 1956 edition of *Aurora Dawn.* In one scene (p. 189) where the business magnate, Talmadge Marquis, is swearing, Wouk uses dashes and in parentheses says: "No matter how the veracity of this scene is lessened, the author will not expose his readers to the rigors of the Marquis vocabulary; even though the United States Supreme Court has ruled that impolite words under certain conditions may become Art." Also see the paragraph in parentheses, p. 228. Earlier he

confesses that the novel "is violating the accepted literary rule of the day, Realism . . . life 'as it really is.' . . . It seems curious that life 'as it really is,' according to modern inspiration, contains a surprising amount of fornication, violence, vulgarity, unpleasant individuals, blasphemy, hatred, and ladies' underclothes" (p. 127). Charles Dickens was quite sensitive about the problem of language as spoken by his gamy characters, e.g. Sikes. In his preface to the third edition of *Oliver Twist* (1841), he wrote: "I saw no reason, when I wrote this book, why the very dregs of life, so long as their speech did not offend the ear, should not serve the purpose of a moral." *Charles Dickens,* ed. Stephen Wall (New York: Penguin, 1970):55.

8. ". . . and dreams give only a vague sort of information in Freud's fashionable revival of Joseph's art" (p. 45). This is a sample not so much of Wouk's anti-Freudianism as it is of what he would regard as the exploitation of Freud's ideas by High Culture. Or: "Not being of the school of literature which deals analytically with the phantasms of slumber, this history makes no effort to follow our hero into the land of Nod, although doubtless the whole truth about him could thereby easily be laid bare under a skilled probe" (p. 62). Also, "Freud as fad" (p. 104). As for the powerful literary critics, Edward Hoagland's essay quotes a New York critic telling Saul Bellow during a political disagreement at a White House reception in what was probably the LBJ administration, "We made you and we can break you." *New York Times* Book Section (4 October 1981):36. See also Norman Podhoretz, *Breaking Ranks: A Political Memoir* (New York: Harper & Row, 1979): 220-30, passim.

9. P. 39. On p. 131, Wouk describes an exchange of glances between Andrew Reale and Carol Marquis as significant "for reasons of the human spirit which could not be fathomed by ten empiric psychologists running a hundred rats through a thousand mazes for ten thousand days." On p. 18 he refers to behaviorists "who say that human beings are soulless bundles of responses to external stimuli."

10. Wouk's knowledge of the Bible and his sense of a recovered religious faith are prominent in the novel. Michael Wilde, the artist-intellectual, foreshadows Noel Airman in *Marjorie Morningstar* and Keefer in *The Caine Mutiny.* Wilde is given the *nom d'occasion* of Bezalel, an Old Testament figure who by divine command built the Tabernacle (Exodus, 31:2; 35:30; 36-38). The world of radio advertising is compared by Wouk to the Valley of Hinnom, outlawed because of idol worship and later known as Gehenna (Joshua, 15:8; 18:16, inter alia). There is a learned reference to Noah as "righteous in his generation" (p. 107). A variant translation (Genesis 6:9) describes Noah as "a just man and perfect in his generations." By "secularist" I mean a philosopher whose system of thought is rationally organized around impersonal and utilitarian patterns and values.

11. P. 107. This value system foreshadows the direction of his fourth novel, *Marjorie Morningstar.* Cf. Henry Miller quoted in 1961 as saying that "civilized peoples don't live according to moral codes or principles of any kind. We speak about them, we pay lip service to them, but nobody believes in them. Nobody practices these rules, they have no place in our lives. Taboos after all are only hangovers, the product of a diseased mind, you might say, of fearsome people who hadn't the courage to live and who under the guise of morality and religion have imposed these things upon us." *Harper's* (September 1981):42, col. 2.

12. Among other serious references are those to Molière, Bishop Berkeley, Aristotle, Plotinus, Marlowe's *Faustus*, Bullfinch, Walt Whitman, Doll Tearsheets, Marley in *A Christmas Carol*, Mozart, and to Pietro Cardinal Bembo, a Medici favorite, particularly of Lucrezia Borgia. The reference to Cervantes is on p.192. Thackeray is known to have reread Cervantes when he was writing *The Newcomes*. Laurence Lerner, *Times Literary Supplement* (5 September 1980):958.

13. So influenced is Wouk by Fielding that, like him, he acts protectively toward his hero, forgetting Kant's philosophy of free will. As Wouk puts it (p. 119), "the human will, while influenced by sensuous circumstances, is not coerced by it," meaning that Reale is responsible for what he is doing. However, later, Wouk exonerates Reale saying that "he knows not what he does, is acting vigorously but innocently according to the values which he has breathed in with the atmosphere of his times" (p. 170).

14. As the novel draws to a close, Wouk reverts to an earlier theme, the godlessness of the present time. He describes the scene of Reale kneeling before the bed-ridden, hospitalized Honey Beaton beseeching her forgiveness. A hundred years ago, says Wouk, the author would have capped such a scene with Scripture: "The Lord is nigh unto the brokenhearted, and will save those of a contrite spirit" (Psalms, 34:18). But, says Wouk, his novel is addressed "to a generation for whom the Lord has been satisfactorily explained away as a cosmic projection of the father-urge. As for the Absolute Unknowable Life Force, what does it care about broken hearts and contrite spirits? It runs the universe unknowably and evolves new life-forms through natural selection, and there an end" (p. 275).

15. Gil Blas de Santillane is referred to by Wouk on p. 170. Lesage, the author of *Gil Blas,* is quoted approvingly in the preface to the first edition of *Aurora Dawn,* reprinted in 1956, p. 9. George Saintsbury regarded Lesage as the inspirer of Fielding and Smollett. The latter translated Lesage's novel into English and, of course, there is the ineffable Mrs. Smollett, the Reverend Stanfield's inamorata in *Aurora Dawn.*

16. P. 269. Zola's famous utterance was published as an article in *Le Figaro* (25 November 1897)—"La vérité est en marche; rien ne peut plus l'arreter."

17. "The Pardoner's Tale" concerns three "young folk" who, during a plague, journey to find Death because he had taken one of their number. An old man says they can find Death under a certain tree. They find the tree and a pile of gold. The three plot against each other so only one can grab the treasure for himself. They succeed in killing each other. Says the Pardoner to the assembly: "Now good men, God foryeve yow youre trespas,/And ware yow fro the synne of avarice." Wouk casts himself as the Pardoner as he quotes (p.176) the Pardoner's preamble: "For though myself be a ful vicious man,/ A moral tale yet I yow telle kan." Chaucer, *Works,* ed. Pollard et al. (London: Macmillan, 1906):145-54 of the *Canterbury Tales.* The distinction between a "moral" and a "literary message" is that the latter "throws an arc light into the far future, whereas a moral casts a candleglow on a small area of the present" (p. 275). The Pardoner's "Latin platitude" is *Radix malorum est cupiditas*—"the root of evil is greed."

3

Caribbean Carnival: A Tragicomedy

There are hundreds of vacation islands and islets in the Caribbean and in the Gulf of Mexico, most of them escape havens for winter-hating residents of North America and Western Europe: white, sandy beaches, endless semitropical sun and sunsets (except for hurricanes and ordinary rainstorms), heroic outdoor sports, haute cuisine (sometimes), privacy or exhibitionism, indoor sports like drinking and/or bed-hopping. As the Ira Gershwin lyrics about the Caribbean had it, "nothing's immoral way out on the coral." It is to one of these islands in the sun, 3,000 miles from New York City, that Wouk turned for the *mise-en-scène* of a tragicomic novel.

During 1965, when Wouk was writing *Don't Stop the Carnival,* he, his wife, and their two sons were living, as they had been for six years, in a large house atop a hill in U.S.-owned St. Thomas, Virgin Islands. It was in this house facing the Caribbean and the Atlantic Ocean that Wouk had written *Youngblood Hawke* and his confession of faith, *This Is My God.*

The novel, however, is not about St. Thomas, as is quite evident from both internal and external details.[1] Officially, the island is called Amerigo; popularly, it is Kinja, the native patois corruption of the once British name, King George the Third Island. The island was acquired by the United States in 1940, Wouk tells us, "as part of the shuffling of old destroyers and Caribbean real estate that went on between Mr. Roosevelt and Mr. Churchill." The island's natives are called Kinjans.

Although there are explosively amusing incidents and smart, rapid-fire Broadway dialogue, the novel is no "escape literature" exercise. The sense of moral crisis rumbles on in the far distance like tropical thunder until in the last chapter there is meaningless, inexplicable death.

On the surface, Kinja is a Caribbean decompression chamber for wearied urban dwellers or younger romantics. Wouk makes it clear, however, that there is no free lunch on this or any other island paradise anymore than there is any free lunch or free anything on the mainland. The sun is hot, the water blue and crystal clear, the air shimmers, and the sand glistens—but man is what he is wherever he is and there is no eluding either reality or illusion. Kinja is more than a haven for urban runaways, it is a backdrop for moral dilemmas. Man takes his contaminations with him wherever he goes.

The novel, Wouk's sixth, takes place in the winter of 1959 when the Caribbean was still an undisputed American *mare nostrum* and Fidel Castro was just a name barely known even to the usually well-informed sources. The novel's protagonist, Norman Paperman, is a Broadway press agent with silvering hair and the lean face of young middle age. He is forty-nine but looks at least five years younger. At the age of fifteen, he fled the family furniture business in Hartford, Connecticut and went to New York where he became the proverbial Manhattanite. His friends, many of them celebrities, were writers, actors, journalists, television people; like himself, semiskilled intellectuals. Most nights he spent at one Broadway restaurant or another, drinking coffee, gossiping. With ironic relish, Wouk describes that life:

> Paperman's circle worked hard at dressing correctly and at reading the right books. Paperman and his friends, indeed, made a second career of being up to the moment and of never wearing, saying, or doing the wrong thing. This was not easy. In New York the right thing to wear or to read, to think or to say, to praise or to blame, can change fast. It can be damaging to miss a single issue of one or another clever magazine. Doctors complain of the flood of periodicals they must read to stay abreast of their profession; but their burden is almost light to that of being a New Yorker like Norman Paperman.

Paperman, whom some people think was modelled after a well-known Broadway publicist of the time named Alan Meltzer, is one of the most fully realized characters in the Wouk oeuvre. The world he inhabits is one which the author had known intimately when, before the war, he was writing comedy scripts for Fred Allen and was himself a gay young blade around town.

Sensitive, elegant, witty, and very much "with it," Paperman had also a radical background. During the 1930s he had been as close to the Communist Party as one could be without paying dues. That era of transcendence arrived during the Spanish Civil War when many liberals and radicals looked upon the Soviet Union as the savior of an embattled Spanish democracy. Orwell's "Homage to Catalonia" came much later as a shock to fellow travelers like Paperman. There are some evocative passages describing the Communist Popular Front period after 1936, and how "that herd of independent minds," to use Harold Rosenberg's phrase, happily conformed to the political orthodoxy of the day, Stalinism.

It is also clear that Paperman is a longtime philanderer. His wife, who had almost joined the Communist Party in her youth as an act of defiance, is aware of Norman's propensity for other bedrooms but they are both devoted parents of Hazel, an attractive nubile girl of nineteen who is in love with her teacher, Sheldon Krug. This young New York University professor of English is married but separated from his wife and child. Krug is also at work, he says, writing a book on Balzac's putative homosexuality.

Norman falls victim first to a heart attack and then to a romantic impulse arising from his disenchantment with Manhattan "and the unutterably narrow weary repetitiousness of the New York life in general, and above all the life of a minor parasite like a press agent." The romantic impulse came upon him when he read a *New Yorker* magazine ad that the Gull Reef Club was for sale on an islet off the bigger isle of Kinja. Paperman's impulse is fulfilled through the intervention of a vulgarian-tycoon Lester Atlas, one-time employer of Paperman's wife, Henny (for Henrietta). Atlas backs Paperman in buying the Gull Reef resort hotel, a sunny spot which, "it suddenly struck Paperman . . . was a place where a Jew had perhaps never before set foot."

On the surface, the novel is a light-hearted tale of Norman's struggles with an Eden which turns out to be a snakepit, ridden by crises, "no-see-'em" sandflies, absconding contractors, eccentric Englishmen, a harmless homosexual Arab merchant, lawyers with dubious ethics, a bartender suffering from an advanced case of satyriasis and gonorrhea, a homicidal handyman, and the general nonstop application of Murphy's law and Adam's curse. Norman finds himself working round the clock but he does get the hotel running.

THE SHATTERING OF THE DREAM

The final dispersal of illusion and impulse for Paperman comes when his tropical dream is finally and totally shattered by the shooting in his bar of the harmless homosexual shopkeeper by an incompetent young policeman. This tragedy is followed, a few moments later, by the accidental auto death of the woman who had been his last romance, a one-time, now faded movie star, Iris Tramm, a divorcee in her thirties.

Iris Tramm demonstrates Wouk's ability to create highly credible and fascinating female characters, a talent he exercises in most of his novels. Iris's Hollywood career is in ruins and she is now the mistress of the island's light-skinned governor, a U.S. appointee. Because it is 1959, racial intermarriage is unthinkable for anyone considering a U.S. political career even if the governor, Alton Sanders, had wanted to divorce his black wife.

Iris has a radical past, similar to that of Norman's wife, although Henny had lost interest in the Communist Party after the Nazi-Soviet Pact in 1939. Iris stayed on until after World War II. Eventually that past had caught up with her in Hollywood and she was finished. It is possible that Wouk based the character of Iris in part on Frances Farmer, a Broadway and Hollywood star who had a short but dazzling career in the late 1930s.

Iris is intrigued with Norman's search for paradise, his fantasy life, the Jewish ex-radical from Manhattan, the all-knowing, wise-guy conversationalist who now wants to be, as his wife teases him, "mine host." Kindly, knowledgeable about the island and its inhabitants, Iris becomes Norman's guide to the realities. While there is still a glamor to Iris, she is addicted to alcoholic binges and to tantrums destructive of all about her and, finally, of herself.

Her relationship with the island governor becomes a test for Paperman the night they first make love at her home. Iris tells him that the governor, her lover, had brought her to the island. This bit of news she had told Norman *en passant* on the assumption that what was well known on the island would be known to Norman. Paperman tries to cover his embarrassment with a dismissive: "Your love life is your own." To which Iris replies:

> "But I love a Negro, dear. Let's get that very straight, I've been in love with him for two years, and it's been beautiful. For a while it was the most beautiful thing that has ever happened to me. Nevertheless, a Negro he is." [Paperman swears that] "it doesn't make the slightest difference."

> "Doesn't it, though? Honestly, now, Norman—all the Broadway and all the Marxism never got three inches below your skin, did it? You're a nice New York Jewish liberal, and you're shocked to the core. Obviously you are."

The evening ends with Iris's dismissal of Norman from her couch. He realizes that he and Iris are going nowhere. It is all too late. Norman loves his shrewd, amusing wife but his short-lived romance with Iris creates a deep emotional tangle. Her death removes the last vestiges of the youth he had been trying to recapture.

QUINTESSENTIAL WOUK

Don't Stop the Carnival is a genial book, quintessential Wouk, an urbane comedy constructed on a scaffolding of bleak truths about youth and middle age, about what Conrad called the "romance of illusions." There is a touch here and there of Anthony Powell and his twelve novels of youth, middle age, and decrepitude (Wouk is a great admirer of Powell). Wouk's novel is beautifully structured and balanced, an entertainment, as Graham Greene might look upon it. If the fortunes of the middle-aged threesome, Iris, Norman, and Henny, end in clear-eyed, unillusioned grimness, there is the promise of an upbeat ending, illusory perhaps, for Hazel, the Papermans' daughter, whose attachment to Professor Klug is deprecated by her parents.

Klug is endowed with most of the characteristics Wouk least likes, reminiscent of Churchill's line, "He has all the virtues I dislike and none of the vices I admire." Klug is a Jew who has abandoned religion for what he calls "paganism." He is vain, pompous, trendy, and a great Freud quoter. There is another young man, a navy frogman who rescues Norman from drowning on his first morning swim along the Kinja reef. The frogman, Bob Cohn, is Klug's antithesis—intelligent, unpretentious, a man of action, inhabiting the navy world where parachute jumps and underwater demolition exercises are routine. Cohn is also taken with Hazel and it becomes clear as the novel ends that the frogman will save Hazel from Klug.

Wouk's intention in writing this novel, as he explained it in his journal, was that "having produced three large-scale novels in a row and each one longer than the last—*The Caine Mutiny*, *Marjorie Morningstar*, and *Youngblood Hawke*—I thought it would be a pleasant change for myself and for my readers if I composed a tale of ordinary length—to be as continuously amusing as possible—kept within the limits of the candidly observed truth which I have tried to make the hall-mark of my fiction."

Then Wouk makes a statement reminiscent of Mark Twain; as he describes the novel: "It is all a lie, as fiction should be, but the picture I have drawn of life in the tropics is as true as I could make it." It was Mark Twain who wrote in Pudd'nhead Wilson's Calendar: "Truth is stranger than fiction; but it is because fiction is obliged to stick to the possibilities; Truth isn't."[2]

NOTES

1. In a newspaper interview after the book's publication (it was a Book-of-the-Month Club selection and a best-seller), Wouk insisted that Amerigo was wholly imaginary, much quieter and more primitive, without any of the big-business bustle of other islands, the hordes of tourists, or ambitious social endeavors of the government in St. Thomas. *San Juan Star* (15 August 1965):9.
2. Quoted in Richard Chase, *The American Novel and Its Tradition* (Baltimore: Johns Hopkins University Press, 1980):143.

4

The Boys of Summer

Ernest Hemingway once said that "all modern American literature comes from one book by Mark Twain called *Huckleberry Finn*."[1] In the same large sense, one might say that all American novelists nurse a secret ambition (and if they do not, they should): to create a modern *Huck Finn*, or even a *Tom Sawyer*, a novel of boyhood about life on the frontier whether in ninteenth-century Mississippi America or in twentieth-century Bronx urban sprawl.[2]

City Boy: The Adventures of Herbie Bookbinder, Wouk's second novel, was published in 1948. Unlike his later novels, this one is anecdotal and episodic rather than being firmly structured, a property which might have encumbered this picaresque narrative.

The story focuses on its fat, 11-year-old hero almost exclusively. The subsidiary characters serve Herbie, a Bronx schoolboy, emerging out of the state of uncorrupted innocence into the tyrannical and untrustworthy world of adults. Herbie is already one of those shrewd and brave youngsters fated to turn upside down those moral lessons propounded by naturally duplicitous parents.

"If I have a favorite creation, to this day, it is the fat little hero, Herbie Bookbinder." So wrote Herman Wouk in a foreword to the 1969 edition of the novel. However, its first edition, twenty years earlier, had sunk almost without a trace. Simon & Schuster, the original publishers, says Wouk, "perhaps convinced that no novel with Jewish characters could sell—this was a general opinion twenty years ago—launched the work as one buries a body at sea." The book received a handful of out-of-town newspaper reviews, was quickly remaindered and went out of print as had *Aurora Dawn*.

A few years later, Wouk published *The Caine Mutiny*. The new publishers, Doubleday, decided to republish *City Boy* on the strength of the *Caine*'s sales, in 1952. While the original publishers had lopped off the full title leaving it with just the two words, *City Boy*, Doubleday restored the full title—*City Boy: The Adventures of Herbie Bookbinder*. The novel was reprinted several times, has been translated into eleven languages, has been selected by book clubs, and been republished in school textbooks and anthologies.[3]

When written without cheap adult jokes, a novel of boyhood can be appealing usually because of the willingness of the reader to identify with the young hero. There is sheer pleasure and some sorrow in watching the expanding consciousness of a prepubescent lad like Herbie, as he begins to move about a world where the contradictions within its moral structure are a permanent provocation to a boy's own moral sense.

The Wouk flair for ambiguity about ethical judgments, to be noted later in *The Caine Mutiny*, is strikingly foreshadowed in *City Boy*. Young Herbie overhears his father say that the combination to the office-safe in his father's Bronx ice factory is Herbie's birthday. Months later in the summer of 1928, Herbie leaves his summer camp on a madcap hitchhiking ride late at night, unbeknownst to the summer camp authorities, to his father's ice factory in order to steal fifty dollars from that very safe. The reason for the "theft" cannot easily be summarized since it involves the highly complicated anthropology of Bronx summer camps in the upper New York State countryside. Suffice it to say that eighth-graders can do the damnedest things when pubescent love and honor are at stake.

The point of this summary is not to emphasize the theft itself. Herbie wrote out a note, unsigned and anonymous, which he was going to leave in the safe informing the victim, his father, that the money would one day be returned with interest to the sum of seventy-five dollars. In his haste to get away, Herbie forgets the note and it remains in his back pocket. However, as Herbie opens the safe to steal the money, he notices a green tin box with his father's initials, J.B. This box contains an important document deeding Herbie's father control of the ice factory stock and thus requiring his approval for the sale of the ice factory, something his partner wants to do but which Herbie's father opposes. The green tin box disappears after Herbie's burglary and when Herbie returns from camp he learns about its disappearance. With good reason, he manages to get into the home of his father's partner—legally, this time—and, sure enough, finds the tin box in a closet.

Here is Herbie's dilemma. To reveal that he knows the whereabouts of the green tin box and its contents means to reveal himself as the thief who stole the fifty dollars, and even going to jail or reform school. Nevertheless, Herbie confesses to his crime in front of his parents and his father's partner, lawyer, and mortgagor; and, because of his theft, he now knows that the tin box is in the possession of his father's partner, an unsavory bit of conspiring by the partner and the mortgagor—who is pressing for the sale of the ice plant. The partner confesses to his misdeed and the sale falls through. Herbie's father is saved. Herbie's honor is saved when the note he forgot to leave in the safe is found by his mother in a trouser pocket, thus confirming his innocent intention.

So all is forgiven but Herbie has to recite the moral lesson, after a solid spanking from his father: "It ain't never right to do bad now and figure to do good later on." In other words, the ends do not justify the means—the fifty-dollars theft could not be justified even though it made possible for Herbie to win the coveted honor of the best camper at Camp Manitou.

Yet the moral lesson is unclear. Had Herbie not stolen the money from his father's safe, he would not have noticed the green tin box with its important documentary contents and Herbie would never have known what to look for and where. And had the box not been found at the crucial moment of the forced sale and transfer of the ice factory at the behest of an unscrupulous mortgagor and the weak-minded partner of his father, Herbie's father would have lost the family business. Without Herbie's theft, the Bookbinders would not have been celebrating the victory of the ice factory at an expensive Bronx restaurant. The eternally complicating variable in the ends/means controversy is the unforeseen consequences of purposive actions by human beings, whether adults or 11-year-old schoolboys.

NOTES

1. In an interview, Wouk echoed this Hemingway aperçu. Said Wouk: "Well, Mark Twain, of course, is the source of modern American writing. *Huckleberry Finn* shows us that we can express everything we have to say in the framework of a very limited vocabulary in the interests of honesty and authenticity." *Book World* (26 December 1971):14. Hemingway is quoted in Richard Chase, *The American Novel* (Baltimore: Johns Hopkins University Press, 1980):139.

2. In the same interview, Wouk was asked whether *City Boy* comes out of the Twain tradition, to which Wouk replied: "Yes, but it's more like *Tom Sawyer*. . . . There's a whole group of first-rate boys' books and, having read them, I guess I wanted to write one." Ibid. Boys' books cited by Wouk were *The Prodigious Hickey, Penrod* , and *Stalky & Co.*

3. The book was purchased by a movie comany which changed Herbie's sex and ethnic origin to an Irish girl, played by Margaret O'Brien, and transformed the Bronx into a Midwestern town and altered the title to *The*

Romantic Age. Says Wouk in the foreword to the new *City Boy* edition: "I did not see it. I have never met anybody who did." The anniversary edition, 1969, carries a highly laudatory preface by John P. Marquand of Wouk who, says Marquand, "is by way of becoming one of the ablest and certainly one of the most sympathetic of our younger writers."

5

The Caine Mutiny: **Authority versus Responsibility**

A month or so before V-J Day and the end of World War II, Lieutenant Herman Wouk, U.S. Naval Reserve aboard the U.S.S. *Southard*, sent a 24-page double-spaced typewritten memorandum addressed to the secretary of the navy. The memorandum was dated 9 July 1945 and the subject was described as: "Reserve Officers, Retention in Fleet of." The enclosure was entitled: "Reluctance of Reserve Officers to Remain in the Postwar Fleet: An Analysis of the Problem and a Suggested Measure." At this time, Wouk was executive officer, i.e., second-in-command of the *Southard*, a destroyer-minesweeper.

On page twenty-one of this memorandum, Wouk wrote: "No topic is more popular in officers' clubs throughout the wide Pacific than 'Captain Bligh' stories of this war." The remedy for "Captain Bligh" commanders, said Wouk in a passage he underlined, was: "Periodic reports shall be made by the officers of a vessel on the quality of the commanding officer. These reports shall not be seen by the commanding officer unless the Navy Dept. desires to bring them to his attention."[1] The theme of the memorandum is to be found in this sentence: "Justifiably or not, young men with a democratic upbringing feel deprived of human dignity and self-respect in our wardrooms today, and military indoctrination does not change that sentiment."[2]

A NONEVENT EVENT

The Caine Mutiny is a novel about an event which never happened in the history of the U.S. Navy, as Wouk is at pains to point out in a prefatory note. It is not the usual disclaimer about "coincidental" resemblances. Between World War I and the aftermath of World War II, there is no record of a court-martial, the novel's climactic scene, resulting from the relief of a ship's commanding officer under articles

184, 185, and 196 of the Naval Regulations. The deposed ship's captain, Queeg, is a fictitious figure, says Wouk, "contrived from a study of psychoneurotic case histories to motivate the central situation and is not a portrait of a real military person or a type." The two captains under whom Wouk served in his three years aboard destroyer-minesweepers were both "decorated for valor," says Wouk.[3]

The novel is divided into seven sections, totaling almost 300,000 words. The first two sections introduce Willie Keith, a young, insouciant, immature civilian as he comes aboard the U.S.S. *Caine*. Beginning with the third part, the scope broadens. Three characters come to share equal importance with Willie at the narrative center—Lieutenant-Commander Queeg and lieutenants Maryk and Keefer. There are two main threads in the novel: Queeg-Maryk-Keefer, a triangle which resulted in a mutiny, and second, the maturing of Willie Keith.

Queeg, a navy regular, i.e. an Annapolis graduate, is neither intelligent, capable, nor amiable. He covers his inadequacy with a fanatic insistence on perfection down to the smallest detail. Such a passion for perfectionism leads to a disastrous and continuing confrontation with the slovenly crew of the *Caine*, an obsolete World War I destroyer demothballed for the war in the South Pacific. Queeg rides Keefer, for whom he has developed a particular dislike. Maryk, the executive officer, develops an admiration for Keefer's intelligence so that when Keefer keeps reiterating the idea that Queeg is a maniac, Mayrk begins to believe it.

A series of episodes, ridiculous and tragic, indicate that Queeg verges on the mentally incompetent. However, the captain has great stores of self-protective cunning and manages to evade responsibility, let alone censure, for his failure as ship's captain. The *Caine* is caught in a typhoon just east of the Philippines one night in December 1944. Not receiving orders to change course and maneuver as necessary to save his ship, Queeg persists in steaming crosswind in obedience to the last orders of the task force commander. The *Caine* is about to founder when Maryk utters the fateful words: "I relieve you, Captain! Mr. Keith, full right rudder." This is legally permissible under Naval Regulations.

Keith is officer of the deck and is confronted with a choice of obeying Maryk or Queeg. He obeys Maryk who then brings the ship safely through the typhoon. The unprecedented incident is hushed up by the navy. Maryk is court-martialed and acquitted by a court, a verdict later criticized by reviewing authorities.

During the court-martial, Keefer shows himself as a coward refusing to criticize the captain as he had done over many months to Maryk and others of the ship's complement. Keefer becomes captain of the *Caine*, after Queeg is transferred to a shore post. Keefer becomes another Queeg. He hides in his cabin working on his novel and conducts the command in the same high-handed manner over niggling details. It is obvious that the aftermath of the court-martial has created for Keefer a sense of his personal inadequacy and lack of support, factors which had plagued Queeg. When the ship is struck by a Japanese kamikaze plane, Keefer jumps overboard. Keith, now the *Caine*'s executive officer, saves the ship by staying aboard and extinguishing the fires. Keefer escapes censure for his cowardice and Keith exonerates him from all blame. The duplication by Keefer of Queeg's contretemps is reminiscent of the opening passage in Karl Marx's *The Eighteenth Brumaire*: "Hegel says somewhere that all great historic facts and personages occur, as it were, twice. He has forgotten to add: the first time as tragedy, the second as farce."[4]

AN UNUSUAL DENOUEMENT

While the novel was an enormous commercial success—a play, a movie, a book club selection[5]—some literary critics and a leading sociologist found the court-martial's extraordinary climax highly objectionable. It is worth considering the implications of this attack on Wouk as a novelist.

Maryk is defended by a Naval Reserve officer-aviator, Barney Greenwald, a successful Jewish lawyer in private life. He has been selected as defense counsel by the Naval District legal officer, whom Greenwald is reluctant to offend even though he dislikes the assignment. Greenwald first demolishes the prosecution's psychiatric testimony favoring Queeg and then Queeg himself on the witness stand in brilliantly withering cross-examinations. Queeg's behavior as he tries to defend himself is so revealing of his incompetence that the acquittal verdict is inevitable.

To celebrate the victory over Queeg,[6] Keefer organizes a champagne celebration for the *Caine* officers at a San Francisco hotel to which Greenwald is pressed to come as guest of honor. Greenwald arrives well after the party has started and is serenaded by the boozy crew with "For He's a Jolly Good Fellow." Pressed for a speech, Greenwald announces that he is drunker than anybody else in the room. Then, in a burst of *in vino veritas* revelation, he tells Keefer, whose $1,000 publisher's advance on his war novel is financing the party, that were he, Greenwald, writing a war novel, he would make Queeg the hero "on account of my mother, little gray-headed Jewish lady." He talks about how the Nazis are "cooking us down to soap over there. . . . I had an uncle and an aunt in Cracow, who are soap now."

Greenwald looks at his now puzzled audience and explains that while he, Keefer, Keith were conducting their civilian affairs, "these stuffy, stupid Prussians, in the Navy and the Army—were manning guns." He then tells Maryk: "You're guilty. . . . I got you off by phony legal tricks—by making clowns out of Queeg and a Freudian psychiatrist—which was like shooting two tuna fish in a barrel." He turns to Keefer: "I defended Steve [Maryk] because I found out the wrong guy was on trial. Only way I could defend him was to sink Queeg for you." He then says: "I'm sore that I was pushed into that spot, and ashamed of what I did, and thass [sic] why I'm drunk. Queeg deserved better at my hands. I owed him a favor, don't you see? He stopped Hermann Goering from washing his fat behind with my mother." He then "toasts" Keefer by throwing the glass of champagne in Keefer's face.

It was this scene which set off loud protests among the critics who derided the whitewash of Queeg and the navy by Greenwald-Wouk. Some years ago, Wouk told an interviewer that when he began *Caine,* he had intended to write a panoramic war novel; instead it became "a novel about authority versus responsibility."[7] In his work journal, he declares the intention of *Caine* "to concretize the hatred of normal young Americans for military life which is mistakenly transferred to the regular military men who symbolize it." He adds: "the crux of the tale will come in the realization of Maryk and Keith that the mutiny was a mistake even though Maryk was acquitted."

Caine, as a novel, was swimming against the tide of World War II, and for that matter, World War I novels, most of which were angry outcries against the military like Mailer's *The Naked and the Dead* and James Jones' *From Here to Eternity.*[8] Wouk's novel accepts the necessity of discipline and authority in a military institution like the navy and, even beyond that, the concept of honor.

CONFLICT OF RIGHT WITH RIGHT

Hegel has written that tragedy is epitomized by "the conflict of right with right." Alasdair MacIntyre has amended that notion by arguing that what makes any protagonist's situation tragic is that, inevitably, he must choose between wrong and wrong. Wouk's inventiveness avoids the pat ending in favor of moral complexities. There are many sides to a human being and Greenwald is no exception. There is almost a mystical intensity as Greenwald delivers his self-castigating speech, a willingness to assume moral responsibility for what he has done. And what he has done has been to force the *Caine*'s officers, the court-martial board, and himself to realize that it is illusory to believe that a ship's captain is a born leader, superior to the mortals around him. And yet it is an essential illusion, without which one might even suggest civilization would founder. One sees the illusion at work in Melville's novella *Billy Budd,* where Captain Vere, who sentences the handsome sailor to hang because he struck and killed the petty officer Claggart, knows that Billy is innocent in spirit.

The two rights in conflict in *Caine* concern the right of a crew and ship to have a decent commanding officer and the right of the navy to prevent the chain of command from being fractured. Or worse, here are two wrongs in confrontation. We accept as the triumph of reason the doctrine of the just war, because with Reinhold Niebuhr we accept the belief that tyranny can be worse than war. What else would justify, except bloodthirsty savagery, resistance to evil by force of arms?

Greenwald wanted to avoid an excruciating dilemma and he told Maryk that he would rather prosecute him than defend him. Before he had taken on the case, he told Maryk that "your sensitive novelist friend is the villain of this foul-up." He tells the naval legal officer in advance of the court-martial that "these men are no underdogs, sir. They deserve to get slugged." There was the fact that while three destroyers foundered, forty stayed afloat in the typhoon and one of them might have been the *Caine,* even with Queeg in command.

Queeg reminds one of a line from Henry James's *The American,* in which Christopher Newman responds to a remark that he looks "dangerous" by saying: "I may be dangerous but I am not wicked."[9] At the court-martial, Queeg is asked by Greenwald to read aloud the fitness reports he had submitted to the naval command on Maryk after all the shenanigans aboard the *Caine* for which he held Maryk responsible. The fitness reports are highly laudatory; Maryk "cannot be too highly commended." There is such a concept as moral ambivalence; things are not always what they seem. The critics who chastised Wouk for the Queeg whitewash were not saying that Greenwald's speech was implausible but that it was morally unacceptable to justify Queeg as compared to Keefer. It is to Wouk's credit that, as a novelist, he has chosen the tough decision and avoided the final judgment.

The now mature Willie Keith, returning to civilian life, writes in a letter home: "Our disloyalty made things twice as tough for Queeg and for ourselves; drove him to his worst outrages and made him a complete psychological mess. . . . Queeg conned the *Caine* for fifteen months, which somebody had to do, and none of us could have done. . . . The idea is, once you get an incompetent ass of a skipper—

and it's a chance of war—there's nothing to do but serve him as though he were the wisest and the best, cover his mistakes, keep the ship going, and bear up."[10]

Even Keefer at the end says: "I feel more sympathy for Queeg than you [Keith] ever will . . . . You can't understand command until you've had it. It's the loneliest, most oppressive job in the whole world. It's a nightmare unless you're an ox."

As a war novel *Caine* has another distinction—the absence of four-letter swearwords, something which other war novels like Jones' *From Here to Eternity* were full of. Granville Hicks made the point that in reading *Caine,* "after a while, you don't notice that the words aren't there." Wouk in a note to the novel on publication wrote: "The general obscenity and blasphemy of shipboard talk have gone almost wholly unrecorded. This good-humored billingsgate is largely monotonous and not significant, mere verbal punctuation of a sort, and its appearance in print annoys some readers."[11]

In his notebooks, Wouk describes how the *Caine Mutiny Court-Martial* came into being. In January 1952, Wouk saw the Broadway presentation of Bernard Shaw's *Don Juan in Hell* which, he said, "was the most electrifying theatrical event to my mind in recent years." It occurred to him that a dramatic reading of a similar kind could be made of the *Caine's* court-martial scene. His idea was to present the scene to Charles Laughton and Paul Gregory, the producers of the Shaw play, for them to edit and produce "thereby making extra money out of work already performed without any additional labor."[12] It is in these notes written two years after the novel's publication that Wouk, having reread his novel, says that "it is in one sense a play of Iago, unmasked, Iago, as Keefer, Greenwald as the unmasker." One cannot press this analogy too far, but one sees here the attempt to create characters who incarnate an idea.

NOTES

1. When the Wouk papers are finally opened, this memorandum will be found in box 5. With the approval of his commanding officer, Wouk forwarded the study directly to the secretary of the navy rather than via the chain of command since, as he put it, "it is an official expression of an individual's idea." Whether Wouk ever received a reply to this memorandum, I do not know. The "Captain Bligh" stories have to do with the commander of H.M.S. *Bounty,* Lieutenant William Bligh, who in 1789 was seized by his mutinous crew and cast adrift with eighteen other crewmen in an open boat. The story became widely known in the United States because of a successful Hollywood movie, *Mutiny on the Bounty,* with Charles

Laughton as Captain Bligh and Clark Gable as the mutiny leader, Fletcher Christian. Laughton later directed the play *The Caine Mutiny Court-Martial*, which Wouk wrote after publication of the novel. The play itself was dedicated to Laughton.

2. This sentence is particularly significant in view of the attack on Wouk by one critic that the author's "antifascism [is] clearly limited to the German enemy" and is unconcerned with the possibility of "fascism" in the United States and its institutions. Joseph J. Waldmeir, *American Novelists of the Second World War* (The Hague: Mouton, 1969):124ff. The writer was attacking *The Caine Mutiny* and James Gould Cozzens's war novel, *Guard of Honor*. Both novels were Pulitzer Prize winners, Wouk's in 1952, Cozzens's in 1948. The influence of a critic on reader taste can be noted in the acknowledgment by Joseph Epstein, editor of the *American Scholar*, that he had "stayed away—wrongly, as I have since discovered—from James Gould Cozzens on the basis of Dwight Macdonald's attack on him in *Commentary* more than 20 years ago." "The Noblest Distraction," *Commentary* 72 (August 1981):52. A change of critical opinion about Cozzens is in the making. See Matthew Bruccoli, *James Gould Cozzens: A Life Apart* (New York: Harcourt Brace, 1983). Bruccoli has written literary biographies of John O'Hara and F. Scott Fitzgerald. See also Jeffrey Hart, "Slumbering Giant," *National Review* (27 May 1983): 632–33, which discusses the Cozzens biography.

3. Although it is not as tangible in *The Caine Mutiny* as it is in his later war novels, Wouk has a tremendous admiration, even veneration, for the navy. In his book about Judaism, for example, he writes: "Possibly because the Navy has meant so much in my life, I have always thought that the Jewish place among mankind somewhat resembles the position of Navy men among other Americans. Are the sailors and officers less American because they are in the navy? They have special commitments and disciplines, odd ways of dress, sharp limits on their freedom. They have at least in their own minds, compensations of glory, or of vital service performed. The Jews are not cut off from mankind by their faith, though they are marked different." *This Is My God* (New York: Pocket Books, rev. ed., 1974):32-33.

4. Karl Marx, *The Eighteenth Brumaire of Louis Bonaparte* in *The Marx-Engels Reader,* ed. Robert C. Tucker (New York: W. W. Norton, 1972):436. Marx is referring to Napoleon's seizure of power on the Eighteenth Brumaire, according to the calendar adopted by the French Revolution, and the coup d'état by Louis Bonaparte, Napoleon's nephew, December 1851, half a century later.

5. Within three years after publication, *Caine* had sold some three million copies in all editions in the United States. Two million copies were sold in Britain, where the book received extraordinarily favorable reviews in serious British weeklies and dailies. The novel has been translated into seventeen foreign languages. The play, *The Caine Mutiny Court-Martial,* based on the book's last part, played to packed Broadway houses for two seasons. (It featured Henry Fonda as Barney Greenwald.) In addition, while Wouk was collecting weather data in Washington, D.C. for the novel, he came across a movie idea about hurricane-hunting pilots, which later became *Slattery's Hurricane*. *Time* (5 September 1955):48.

6. "There must be some superstition about the letter 'Q,' ' David Lodge has written, "so many nasty, malicious, detestable characters in literature have names that begin with it." *Times Literary Supplement* (20 February 1981):186. He cites Quilp in *The Old Curiosity Shop*, Quint in *The Turn of the Screw*, to which one might add Quasimodo in Hugo's *The Hunchback of Notre Dame*, the scheming widow Quin in *Playboy of the Western World* and, of course, the politico-literary symbol of World War II and thereafter, Quisling. An onomastic study of the letter Q in literary names might also comment on the relationship between Queequneg on the whaler, *Pequod*, a ship of outcasts driven by the monomaniacal Captain Ahab, and Queeg.

7. *Publisher's Weekly* (7 February 1972):44.

8. Among academic critics of the whitewash scene are W.J. Stuckey, *The Pulitzer Prize Novels: A Critical Backward Look* (Norman: University of Oklahoma Press, 1966):158-64; William H. Whyte, *The Organization Man* (New York: Doubleday Anchor, 1956), ch. 19; Harvey Swados, "Popular Taste and 'The Caine Mutiny,' " *Partisan Review* 20 (March-April 1953):248-56.

9. Henry James, *The American* (Boston: Houghton Mifflin, Riverside Ed., 1962):363.

10. In his notebooks, Wouk quotes a commentary on Samuel 2:13 from the Old Testament by Rashi, a noted eleventh-century exegist: "Jephthah in his time, as Samuel in his time; the meanest leader, once set over you, must have your loyalty as though he were the noblest of the noble."

11. Granville Hicks, "The Novel Isn't Dying," *New Leader* (10 December 1951):23. On one page of Wouk's notebook on *Caine*, there is a sentence in capital letters: "Cut every single bit of foul language in the book. We did it. So can you." It is signed: Dumas, Stevenson, Tolstoi, Twain, Conrad, Defoe. Below these signatures, is another line: "Don't listen to them," signed, Smollett.

12. Laughton convinced Wouk that a "reading" of the court-martial scene would not work on the stage unlike *Don Juan in Hell* which did, and "that I would have to write a play. The whole effort, start to finish, constituted a year's interruption in the writing of Marjorie Morningstar." Letter from Wouk in my possession.

6

Bewitched, Bothered, and Bewildered:
Marjorie Morningstar

Although Wouk's fourth novel was not published until 1955, ideas for such a work were germinating as early as 1940, then again in 1947, and finally in 1950-52 when he began its composition. In July 1940 he wrote a playlet titled "Crisis over Marjorie," which had two performances as a benefit for the United Jewish Appeal. In a handwritten note found among his papers and dated 11 June 1952, Wouk described the playlet as one which "marked my first effort in adult years to write seriously after six postcollege years as a gagman. As such it was crucial. Crude and flat though it is, it surely contained a vital spark to haunt me for twelve years and force itself up again as a novel—though how good a novel I can't yet say." This 20-page one-acter, Wouk wrote in this note, was one of "several milestones in my writing career."[1]

The scene of the playlet, as of the novel, was what Wouk called "the pleasant ghetto," bounded on the east by Central Park West, on the west by West End Ave. (where Wouk had lived with his family during 1932-36), north by 110th St. and south by West 72d St. A number of the themes in the novel appear in primitive form in "Crisis over Marjorie." The father and mother, here called Lippman, are concerned over Marjorie—a 20-year-old Barnard junior—and her social life, and the risk of seduction at the hands of a jaunty sculptor, Noel Stern. He is exposed as a wife deserter by the Jewish lawyer whom the Lippman family would like her to marry. Noel Stern's real name turns out to be Nathan Steinberg in the playlet.[2]

Noel Stern, twenty-five, is the intellectual *manqué,* a character who seems to surface throughout Wouk's novels: Klug in *Don't Stop the Carnival,* Keefer in *The Caine Mutiny,* Michael Wilde in *Aurora Dawn* and Noel Airman, born Saul Ehrmann in *Marjorie Morningstar.*

The early Noel Airman wrote and read poetry, studied at the Sorbonne after a year at New York University. In a sense Airman is not an intellectual concerned with values and ideas as he is a manipulator for the pleasure of manipulating people or, perhaps, he is an old-fashioned bohemian who exemplifies the spirit of *épater le bourgeois*.

Marjorie fancies herself to be somewhat of an artist because she dreams of being a famous actress and her name no longer Morgenstern but Morningstar. It is 1933 and Marjorie, a student at Hunter College, a free municipal institution, has just had a triumph at a Columbia College dance: the belle of the ball. Although in his work journal Wouk was at the outset critical of Marjorie, his feelings toward her changed considerably as the novel progressed.

In a discussion with Wouk in 1980, I asked him how he felt about Marjorie a quarter of a century later. Did he like her?

> The fact is, I fell in love with her, for all her faults. And I did not consider her a "vapid monster" at all, when the portrait was done, but an "Everygirl." At least that was my working idea. Marjorie is a novel of historical interest; it is a story of the way we were. The Marjorie story is about a world that is lost forever. The framework in which Marjorie operates no longer exists. It is timebound. This is true of any long-lived novel. For instance, adultery for Anna Karenina meant the destruction of a woman; today it is a difficult episode, if that, in modern marriage. Nevertheless as soon as you are thirty pages into Tolstoy's book, you accept the premises. And you go on from there responding to that set of premises.
>
> Most of the heroines in Trollope's novels are girls who live by a rigid framework as Marjorie Morningstar does. Either they get their man or they are done for. We go on reading Trollope, though the framework is of another era. Well, into the framework of the new freedom in the 1950s erupted a 600-page book about a girl losing her virginity. It was risky to write a book like that at such a time. I was keenly aware of it. Yet thirty years later, the book lives on.
>
> It is especially widely read by girls as they grow up.[3] And I get letters from them, but the age level keeps dropping, curiously. A girl's giving up her virginity is a drastic turn in her life. It is a universal experience, an experience that will never die in its consequences no matter how modern freedoms have blurred it.

A CONTROVERSIAL NOVEL

Marjorie Morningstar is much more than the story of a middle-class Jewish girl who, raised in the Jewish tradition, tries to escape it. And it is more than a tale about the deflowering of a beautiful 21-year-old girl, who never loses her guilt about her affair with Airman. The novel quickly became controversial among Jewish publicists and religious figures and among secular intellectuals.

Marjorie Morningstar was, at the time of its publication, a rarity among novels in that it was dealing directly and specifically with the

Jews of New York and how they moved about from one urban
neighborhood to another—from the Bronx to Central Park West and
then to Park Avenue—as part of Jewish upward mobility. Among its
predecessors were Ludwig Lewisohn's *The Island Within* and Abraham Cahan's *The Rise of David Levinsky*. While there are a good many
Jewish novelists, few dealt with the kind of Jewish themes that Wouk
did.

Marjorie Morningstar was the first Jewish novel that was popular
and successful, not merely to a Jewish audience but to a general one.
There had been other Jewish novels earlier in the century by such
authors as Charles Angoff, Michael Gold, Ben Hecht, Maurice Samuel,
Henry Roth, and Daniel Fuchs. These were generally unsuccessful
novels, although Roth and Fuchs received critical acclaim. Publishers
had become reluctant to publish novels on Jewish themes because of
their lack of success in terms of sales. No better proof of the novel's
appeal to a general audience can be offered than the fact that *Marjorie*
was chosen as a Book-of-the-Month Club selection. But serious critics
were split about the quality of the novel, particularly the way in which
Wouk dealt with Jewish themes.

Angry Clergy, Angry Critics

Leslie Fiedler and Norman Podhoretz were particularly sharp about
Wouk's treatment of the Jews of New York City. Jewish clergy were
also angered by the novel. And yet looking back more than a quarter
century later, it is hard to see why.

For Fiedler, *Marjorie* was "the first fictional celebration of the mid–
twentieth century détente between the Jews and middle-class America;
and the movie which has followed, the *Time* story and the *Time* cover
picture are, in effect, public acknowledgements of that fact." There is a
certain truth to this insight. Fiedler feels that the high literature of
Western writers shows the Jew as seeming to represent the common
human lot, man's fate in the modern world, rootless, alienated, terror-
ized, and exiled. This view, rooted in the notion of alienation, so dear
to the "new sensibility," is combatted by Wouk, whose Jews are not
metaphors or symbolic variables in a literary theory. There is no
indication why it is a particularly heinous sin to have established such a
détente, if indeed it exists. However, Fiedler's view of this détente
between Jews and middle-class America, if so understood by literary
critics and literary intellectuals, could explain a good deal of the
animosity felt by high-culture critics toward Wouk.

Fiedler traces a relationship between Samuel Richardson's *Clarissa
Harlowe* and *Marjorie Morningstar,* through the mediating force of
Flaubert "who has taught Wouk . . . what middle-class life has

become, what dreams and frustrations the daughters of Clarissa have inherited since the bourgeois revolution has been converted into business-as-usual." For Clarissa has become Madame Bovary, a "truth" which Wouk stubbornly will not confess to, says Fiedler. In Wouk's novel the seducer Noel Airman is the modern counterpart of Robert Lovelace in *Clarissa,* "whose struggle with the immovable Clarissa all Europe once followed through a million words."

There is a good deal of mischief and deliberate misunderstanding of Wouk's intention. The novel, says Fiedler, offers a counterview, namely that the "Jew was never (or is, at least, no longer) the rootless dissenter, the stranger which legend has made him, but rather the very paragon of the happy citizen at home, loyal, chaste, thrifty, pious and moderately successful—in short, not Noel Airman but Marjorie Morningstar!"[4]

Not merely from talking with Wouk, as I have, but from any but the most careless misreading of the novel, it should be clear that the author has sympathy and sad affection rather than admiration for Marjorie, even though as a married woman she keeps a kosher home and two sets of dishes. Wouk's viewpoint is far more that of Wally Wronken, the young adult camp sketch writer who worshipped Marjorie from afar when they were in their late teens. Wally, successful writer and playwright, runs into Marjorie, 39 years old when the novel ends, mother of two, an exurbanite, and now "the sweet-natured placid gray mama she has turned into." If anyone speaks for the author it is Wronken when he says that "the only remarkable thing about Mrs. Schwartz [Marjorie] is that she ever hoped to be remarkable."[5]

In a critique of Fiedler, Irving Howe described Fiedler's book from which I have quoted, *Love and Death in the American Novel,* as destined "to become a classical instance of sophisticated crankiness." Many of Fiedler's statements, says Howe, "have little to do with literature and even less with that scrupulous loyalty to a work of art which is the critic's primary obligation."[6]

Podhoretz, today editor of *Commentary* magazine, publication of the American Jewish Committee, was at the time he wrote the review in 1956, beginning a career as a literary and cultural critic. He made some wild misstatements about Wouk's intentions, leaving the impression that he, like Fiedler, saw in the novel a *Weltanschauung* which Wouk, in fact, repudiated. However, after some sharp comments about the novel, Podhoretz said quite rightly: "*Marjorie* is, after all, a Jewish book, perhaps the first novel to treat American Jews intimately as Jews without making them seem exotic." The title of the review itself foreshadowed the analysis—"The Jew as Bourgeois." Podhoretz is unforgiving about Wouk's subtleties in depicting Marjorie's trapped existence. Since the author does not macerate what Podhoretz calls "all the vulgarities and accidental accretions of American Jewish life," then he must be for them, a wedding at a fancy Fifth Avenue hotel in New York catered by some exhibitionistic vulgarians named Lowenstein and the suburban kaffeeklatsch.[7]

The Jewish novel must have been such a rarity that Marjorie, lacking any contemporary counterparts, seemed fated to be misunderstood. (One could easily show that Wouk was appalled at what might be called ersatz Judaism.) Such misapprehension may explain why one rabbi actually called Wouk anti-Semitic; the novel, he complained, did not contain a single Jewish character who was anything but gross and vulgar.[8] Some of these critics seemed more informed by a spirit of religious Comstockery than by a willingness to understand Wouk's aim.

Apologia Pro Sua Marjorie

Wouk was so taken aback that in 1959, when he published *This Is My God,* he wrote that in *Marjorie Morningstar* "I did my best to portray a bar-mitzva with accuracy and with affection. I thought I succeeded pretty well, but for my pains I encountered the most bitter and violent objections from some fellow Jews. I had, they asserted, made a sacred occasion seem comical. There were comic touches in the picture, of course, but I believe these lay in the folkway as it exists, not in the imagination of the writer."[9]

The novel was strongly defended in one magazine, *Jewish Life,* where the writer said that Wouk had depicted in the novel "a negation of all the authentic qualities of Jewish faith . . . the nadir of a half century of slow erosion, and of cultural and spiritual assimilation." Maxwell Geismar had written in his review of the book that this cultural and spiritual assimilation was the culmination of "the tragicomic meeting of traditional Jewish culture and the American success myth. The children abandon the best part of their heritage in order to take on the worst aspects of the new environment." *Jewish Life* agreed totally with this statement.[10]

A DEFENSE OF WOUK

One of the more interesting essays on the novel by Professor Joseph Cohen compared Wouk's novel with Hemingway's *The Sun Also Rises.* Marjorie is a Jewish version of Lady Brett Ashley, and Noel Airman, the typical Hemingway expatriate and a composite of Jake Barnes and Robert Cohn. Professor Cohen says that Jewish critics of Wouk, like Charles Angoff, fail to recognize that

Wouk, in addition to being a devout Orthodox Jew, is a conscientious
artist writing in as much a recent American tradition, popularized by
Hemingway, as he is writing in an older Jewish one . . . .

Hebraism flourishes here above all else, and if the customs and ceremonials are portrayed unsympathetically as many believe they have been, it
is not because Wouk subconsciously seeks alienation from a faith he no
longer believes in, but rather because he wants to remove the taint of
human corruption from the idealism implicit in the symbolism of the
ceremonials.[11]

Angoff, to whom Professor Cohen refers, had an extraordinary
change of heart between (December) 1955, when he wrote in the
Hadassah Newsletter, and 1970, when he wrote an introduction to two
extracts from *Marjorie Morningstar* in a collection of American Jewish
literature. In the Hadassah publication he wrote that *"Marjorie
Morningstar* is the type of novel one had hoped had disappeared from
the American literary scene." Angoff called the novel "mean-spirited
. . . filled with vulgar and offensive Jews . . . filled with the mockery of
Jewish customs."

In a reader called *The Rise of American Jewish Literature,* there are
two extracts from *Marjorie Morningstar*—"The Seder" and "The Man
She Married." There is an introduction to these extracts which describes Wouk's novel as having "really catapulted interest in Jewish
material to a lofty high." Wouk's portrait of a Seder "best epitomizes,
out of all the typical material in the novel, the author's double view, in
which the realistic rendition of certain vulgarities is paralled by a
feeling for certain simple souls." The Seder scene shows "the partial
breakdown of this ancient family rite in American Jewish homes; not a
pleasant picture, and surely not a total one, but there is truth in it."[12]

The man who wrote this introduction was Charles Angoff, coeditor
with Meyer Levin of this collection of American Jewish literature. No
longer was Angoff hoping for the disappearance of this type of literature "from the American literary scene." This same critic, fifteen years
later, was helping in its perpetuation.

DEALING WITH "NOVEL NOVELS"

What is one to make of all this brouhaha among the critics? Marjorie
is Madame Bovary; no, she is Clarissa Harlowe; no, she is Lady Brett
Ashley. One is tempted to agree with Denis Donoghue when he writes:
"Literary theory is not a science; it is best understood as a rhetoric."
Marjorie is no Bovary. She may have had, like Emma Bovary, her
romantic fantasies but unlike Emma, who cannot stand living in a small
Normandy town married to an unromantic doctor, Marjorie is happy to

be living in Mamaroneck, a New York exurb, married to a lawyer and leading a contented existence. Marjorie could not possibly commit suicide. And she is hardly a Clarissa, either literally or symbolically, any more than Noel Airman is a Robert Lovelace nor has he the stuff of the emasculated Jake Barnes. Airman is a coward, not a Hemingway hero, and there is no content to Airman's expatriation which, anyway, is quite brief and meaningless. And what kind of critical responsibility is it when Leslie Fiedler attacks Wouk for having managed "to write about love without mentioning the sexual organs"?[14]

What is suggested by these wild outbursts, these flights of the critical imagination, is that many modern literary critics have a terrible time dealing with "novel novels," i.e., traditional novels, the bases of which are narrative mode and naturalism. One wonders what a Leslie Fiedler of Dickens's time would have written with the seriatim publication of *Pickwick, Oliver Twist,* or *Nicholas Nickleby,* between 1836 and 1838.

Marjorie and Noel Airman are both quite believable characters, standing on their own within the Jewish context, even possibly outside that context. Jews have no monopoly on ordinary young women who want to be famous but lack the talent, will, or courage to achieve that fame, and thus finally settle down to an ordinary human existence—a rather antiromantic conclusion, messy, untidy like the upheaval of a beach after the typhoon.

Wouk brought the news, and it was all bad, that the Jewish princess was not going to get home free. And as happened to the messenger who brought Cleopatra the news that Mark Antony had married another: "I'll unhair thy head. Thou shalt be whipp'd with wire, and stew'd in brine, smarting in lingering pickle"—the literary intellectuals tried to do this to Wouk, but as noted in the case of Charles Angoff, fifteen years later it was another story.

Carlyle once said that the critic's first and only duty is to uncover "what the poet's aim really and truly was, how the task he had to do stood before his eye, and how far, with such materials as were afforded him, he has fulfilled it."[15] The storm over Wouk's novel reveals more about the low level of criticism in literary America in the 1950s than it does about the novel itself.

NOTES

1. Box 14 of the Wouk papers at Columbia University Library. In this box is a handwritten title page of the novel on a much yellowed lined sheet; it is dated 6 November 1950. *Aurora Dawn* also started out as a play (see ch. 2). In his journal, Wouk also writes: "Don't deprive yourself of the breadth

and intimacy of the novel by thinking of that damned lighted platform and those damned actors."

2. The mimeographed text of the playlet is to be found in a box with the label "Memorabilia and Pre-War Navy."

3. Linda Ronstadt, the singing star, described her reaction in reading *Marjorie Morningstar* while still a teen-ager: "In retrospect, it was terrible for a young girl—it screwed me up about love and romance and everything. But I loved it then, and it made me wish I was Jewish." *Washington Post* (4 May 1978).

4. Leslie Fiedler, *Love and Death in the American Novel* (New York: Criterion, 1960):41, 249, 250, 252.

5. *Marjorie Morningstar*, ch. 48—"Wally Wronken's Diary"—is a final summation of the author's view of the heroine. The quotations are on p. 756 of the paperback edition.

6. Irving Howe, "Literature on the Couch," *Celebrations and Attacks: Thirty Years of Literary and Cultural Commentary* (New York: Harvest/HBJ book, 1979):150, 153.

7. Norman Podhoretz, "The Jew As Bourgeois," *Commentary* 30 (February 1956):186–88. Another Jewish novelist who has had his problems with critics, secular and religious, is the gifted Canadian writer Mordecai Richler. His classic *The Apprenticeship of Duddy Kravitz* as well as his more recent and picaresque novel, *Joshua Then and Now* are superb examples of this genre dealing with Jewish life in the Montreal "ghetto," Richler's home town.

8. Probably the two most vicious attacks were by Maurice Samuel, "Not Simply Rubbish," *Midstream* (n.d.):92–98, and Rabbi Mortimer Cohen, *Philadelphia Jewish Exponent* (1 January 1960). A more sorrowful than angry open letter by the editors of *Synagogue Service* (n.d.) criticized Wouk for making a mockery of the Seder! According to Irwin Ross, Wouk was attacked in such Jewish publications as *Congress Weekly, Jewish Spectator, and American Judaism*, shortly after the novel's publication. Irwin Ross, *New York Post* (22 January 1956):2M.

9. *This Is My God*, p. 113.

10. Emanuel Feldman, "Marjorie Morningstar and the Intellectual," *Jewish Life* (March-April 1956):47. Maxwell Geismar reviewed the novel in the *New York Times* Book Review (4 September 1955):1.

11. Joseph Cohen, "Wouk's Morningstar and Hemingway's Sun," *South Atlantic Quarterly* 57 (Spring 1959):222.

12. *The Rise of American Jewish Literature*, ed. Charles Angoff and Meyer Levin (New York: Simon & Schuster, 1970): 511. The junior editor of this reader had reviewed *Marjorie Morningstar* in the *Saturday Review of Literature* quite favorably (3 September 1955):9.

13. Denis Donoghue, "The Onward March of Obsolescence," *Times Literary Supplement* (11 July 1980):775.

14. Fiedler attacked Wouk in the *New Leader*, quoted in *New York Post* (16 January 1956):38.

15. Quoted in H.L. Mencken, "Criticism of Criticism of Criticism," *Prejudices: A Selection* (New York: Vintage, 1959):5.

7

Youngblood Hawke: "Young Man from the Provinces"

Youngblood Hawke, Wouk's fifth novel, was the writer's daring breakthrough. The novel, written between October 1957 and December 1961, represented a tremendous leap from relatively simpler and undemanding novel structures to a vastly more complicated and more ambitious development of plot and character.[1]

The 878-page novel (the paperback) is replete with richly detailed subplots and counterplots. It is animated by a sociocultural sweep not to be found in Wouk's four earlier novels.[2] *Youngblood Hawke* was the novelist's test, his "try out." If he could bring this off, he could then go to work, as he wrote in his journals, on his projected war novels which at the time went by their code names in these journals as Gog and Magog, the symbolical enemies in *Revelation* (XX: 7-9).

"WRITERS ARE THE WORLD'S DULLEST PEOPLE"

Wouk was quite conscious of one problem while he was writing the novel. He noted in his journal (and every word was capitalized): "Writers are the world's dullest people. Their problems are the world's dullest problems and the world wants another novel about a writer somewhat less than it wants a hydrogen war." In another paragraph he added: "This novel must be written in constant awareness of that fact."

A second problem is to satisfy a reader that a man, described by the author as a genius writer, is actually so. In a historical novel, the events and personages are known to the reader in some detail. While their treatment is fictional, valuations placed by the author upon the personages are usually mediated by some previous historical assessment of which the reader is surely aware.

In a *Kunstleroman* about a purely imaginary character, the reader has to take the author's word that the hero has really written great novels, painted great canvases, or composed great symphonies. The solution to that problem for Wouk was somewhat complicated: "His effect upon people is the real way to know he is great because I can't write his books for him." However, in another journal entry he added: "But this is not a novel about a writer. It is the tale of a great man riding through Araby on a magic carpet of talent and crashing to an early death."[3]

Youngblood Hawke is a gargantuan tale about the short and unhappy life and times of a self-styled Kentucky mountain boy who barges into New York with The Novel. In Lionel Trilling's typology, it is the tale of the Young Man from the Provinces. Youngblood is the young provincial, the postulant in the tradition of Stendhal's *The Red and the Black*, Balzac's *Père Goriot* and *Lost Illusions*, Flaubert's *Sentimental Education*, Tolstoy's *War and Peace*, Dostoyevsky's *The Idiot*. Jean-Jacques Rousseau, says Trilling, "is the father of all the Young Men from the Provinces, including the one from Corsica."[4]

The Young Man from the Provinces need not, in a literal sense, be a provincial, although in Youngblood's case, he is. Unawed by the big city, he is going to seize it by storm. Atop the Empire State Building, where he is taken shortly after his arrival in New York by a Broadway producer, Youngblood exlaims: "I love this city; I'll never leave it and I'll lick it."

While the novelist lacks the right establishment connections or any aristocratic or other ascriptive status, he is certain that he will win everything by his talent, intellect, good looks, bravado, iconoclasm, and self-assurance of his destiny which he will communicate to others, especially to beautiful and intelligent women. Yet despite his early good fortune, the Young Man from the Provinces is doomed—the poet *maudit*, the poet cursed.[5]

The novel is a long, complex love story concerning Arthur Youngblood Hawke, writer. By the time he dies in 1953 at the age of thirty-three, he has in seven years written five major works, has become an international celebrity, hovered on the brink of financial destruction, and has been involved with two women, Frieda Winter, the aging mistress and a figure in New York's commercial culture, and Jeanne Greene, a book editor fated to love but never marry Youngblood.[6]

LITERARY INFLUENCES

Balzac's Life First Stirred Wouk's Imagination

Wouk has said that the original impulse for the novel was Balzac's career, "a talented man driven by his ambition, his women, and his greed." Not satisfied with the results of his writing, Balzac speculated outside his literary career and the results were his financial ruin. Trying desperately to repay his debts, Balzac wore himself out by more writing.[7] Wouk took this impulse and merged it with literary life in New York in postwar America. While there are touches from the lives of other writers besides Balzac—Thomas Wolfe, Charles Dickens, Jack London, Mark Twain, Theodore Dreiser, and others—Youngblood is a character who stands out as a unique creation in modern American fiction.

Youngblood is the epitome of solipsism; nothing, for him, exists outside of himself and his genius. The world outside exists only as a reflection of his existence, his problems, and eventually, his desperation. The world, inescapable in Wouk's earlier novels as well as the later ones, is escapable for Youngblood. For him, "the outside reality" mattered as it did to Baudelaire, "provided that it helps me feel that I am what I am."[8] What makes *Youngblood Hawke* so vital and endlessly fascinating is the enormous amount of observation by the author of society in general and literary society in particular.

One of the most dramatic and premonitory moments in the novel occurs quite early, almost at the beginning of the book at a literary party for Youngblood. Karl Fry, the ex-Communist who, in the course of the story, will give the names of his former comrades to a Congressional inquiry committee, delivers an extraordinary apostrophe. It is not often, says Fry to the glittering assembly which has come to meet the new culture hero, that one is invited "to the running of a stag," a reference to the poem "A Runnable Stag" by a little-remembered Scottish poet, John Davidson, who committed suicide in 1909. Fry takes Davidson's conceit about the barbarous custom in British hunting society and transforms it into a malevolent prediction about Hawke's end as "a runnable stag, a royal beast, and running it to death was a pleasure for rich men. . . . The ladies loved it, too, running the big male thing to death."

When Fry finishes his dramatic paraphrase of the Davidson poem ("And a gamekeeper pulled its head back by its branching horns, took out a sharp knife and offered the loveliest lady in the party the cutting of the stag's throat"), Hawke breaks the silence and asks whether the stag ever outran his pursuers and lived to a ripe and royal old age. "I don't know anything about stag hunting," Fry tells him. "I believe he occasionally did. But you won't, Youngblood Hawke." Hawke disbelieves Fry because, says Wouk in a journal note, "the point is he's a stag, though he thinks he's a hunter."

Joyce's Notion of the Epiphany

I single out this episode of the novel because it illustrates James Joyce's notion of the epiphany, so strikingly defined by Steven Marcus, as "that moment in a narrative when meaning is suddenly revealed or shown forth, when everything that has gone before is abruptly flooded with sense and significance, and when everything that comes after is profoundly and unalterably affected by the significance that has been revealed."[9]

Wouk's work journal kept during the writing of *Youngblood Hawke* is a fascinating view into the mind of a novelist heedful, perhaps, of the last sentence in Henry James's preface to *The Princess Casamassima*: ". . .something like *this* wisdom—that if you haven't, for fiction, the root of the matter in you, haven't the sense of life and penetrating imagination, you are a fool in the very presence of the revealed and assured; but that if you *are* so armed you are not really helpless, not without your resource, even before mysteries abysmal."[10]

Wouk's great concern was whether he could handle a "double plot of this complexity," whether he could enlarge his "scope so as to deal in detail with imagined and invented characters giving them life details from people around me far from them. I certainly must be able to do this to attempt a Biblical novel or a Leyte Gulf. This is breaking new ground with a vengeance."[11]

The Wolfe-Dreiser Matter

Overhanging Wouk as he planned and "executed" *Youngblood Hawke* were the novels by Thomas Wolfe and Theodore Dreiser, whose leading characters and plots he regarded as inept and unconvincing but nevertheless important in American literature. In one journal entry, he wrote: "I don't believe I'm condemned to Dreiser," by which he means that he has made the following progress: "the transition from imitation literary in *Aurora Dawn* and *City Boy* to straight [W. Somerset] 'Maugham' in *Slattery's Hurricane* [Hollywood film script] and *The Caine Mutiny* which evolved into Dreiser in *Marjorie Morningstar*." For Wouk, *Youngblood* represented his hope "to achieve if I can a significant break in style."[12]

To assist in moving to new ground, Wouk created for himself a different approach to plot construction to which he gave the code name Babar, after the narrative technique in the children's books by Laurence de Brunhoff. This approach meant the development of a compact, rapid narrative style bringing each episode to a narrational point and compressing a large series of happenings into a small compass. Wrote Wouk in another entry: "One thing Dreiser never achieved was Babar." His main advantage over Dreiser, he says, "besides humor and a better heart, [is] the power to edit my work." And when it came to editing, Wouk says of the manuscript: "The job of the first 1,300 pages is to reduce Dreiser to Babar."

Regarding Wolfe, Wouk asks himself: "What the hell do you know about Southerners?" And he answers: "Well, I'm *not* going to do it about Jews, and if it suffers in the depth and accuracy, let it suffer. I'm supposed to be a man of imagination, not the Jewish James T. Farrell."[13] His capsule summary of *Youngblood* is "Balzac plus Wolfe, mainly, plus the kind of corporate litigation that fills the land—I must do it as well as I can, and take what pasting I must for tone." His sensitivity about the Balzac-Wolfe combination is evident in another entry: "The whole idea of grafting Balzac's career on Wolfe's origins is a very queer one and will go down hard with my dear pals, the critics, but to hell with them."

WRITERS AND AUDIENCE

Wouk rejects the solution to plot construction by Balzac and Dreiser which for them meant "to write it all out as honestly as possible and damn the readers; let them read it if they could. Dreiser paid the penalty. People don't read *The Financier* and *The Titan,* crammed with the best American fiction writing outside Twain. These books, it is true, had another great flaw, a frigid and repellent hero. But that effect was part of Dreiser's headlong preoccupation with money and power in the story. Balzac's money novels pay the same penalty."

One can offer as a verdict on *Hawke* that it is a superb study of New York publishing circles and of how literature is merchandised into bestsellers, Broadway plays, and Hollywood epics. It is also an effective drama depicting the price which must be paid for sins, mortal or venial, by such a mighty force, an energumen like Youngblood Hawke. He had his moment at the New York strutter's ball and went on to become another memory.

There are not many American novels about writers. Budd Schulberg's *The Disenchanted,* about Fitzgerald; Meredith Nicholson's *The Poet,* about James Whitcomb Riley; George Webber in

Wolfe's *You Can't Go Home Again*. What Wouk has achieved is the creation, through the fluency of his adaptive imagination, of a major character in a challenging genre.

NOTES

1. Wouk started writing this novel 18 October 1957, the day after the unsuccessful Broadway opening of a comedy satire, *Nature's Way*. He completed it four years later taking out eighteen months in that period to write his religious testament, *This Is My God*. In his work journal, he wrote: "I view Hawke, like Caine and Marjorie, as an experimental reaching out for broader powers and new tools." Work journals, box 1, "Youngblood Hawke."
2. New York City is the locale of *City Boy, Aurora Dawn,* and *Marjorie Morningstar*. To a lesser extent, New York is the locale for *Don't Stop the Carnival,* looking upon the Caribbean island as an extension of the city. In the first two novels the city is little more than backdrop. In *Marjorie* the city is important, but it is really only the Jewish New York of the 1950s. In *Youngblood* New York is as important a part of the story as Paris is to the world of Balzac; other places, Hollywood, Kentucky, Europe, seem to be tributaries of New York.
3. Balzac was fifty-one when he died, Thomas Wolfe thirty-eight, F. Scott Fitzgerald forty-four, Nathanael West thirty-seven, George Büchner, author of the still-played *Danton's Death,* died at twenty-four. Heinrich von Kleist, the early–nineteenth-century playwright and short-story writer, committed suicide at thirty-four.
4. Lionel Trilling, *The Liberal Imagination* (New York: Viking, 1950): 61ff. In his essay on James's *Princess Casamassima,* Trilling calls Hyacinth Robinson, the Young Man from the Provinces, "this child-man," an apt description for Wouk's hero.
5. Thomas Chatterton, who committed suicide at seventeen, was a poet *maudit,* one about whom Alfred de Vigny wrote a drama. *Les Poètes maudits* was a series of biographical studies by Paul Verlaine about his fellow Symbolists.
6. There are several autobiographical resemblances between Youngblood and Wouk—three years in the World War II navy in the South Pacific; admiration for the same writers, such as Dickens and Mark Twain; writing plays during odd moments while on naval duty; publishing a best-selling World War II novel; both writing a smash Broadway hit play; working in Hollywood for a time; unhappy involvement in "money situations" (Wouk's phrase).
7. Wouk's journal makes clear that Youngblood is related to Lucien de Rubempré, one of the protagonists in Balzac's "Scènes de la vie de province" from his *Comédie humaine*. Part 2 of the novel is titled "Un Grand Homme de province à Paris." Lucien leaves Angoulême, a small town in western France, to make his name as a poet in Paris. He finds the Parisian literary world corrupt. He falls in with the master criminal Vautrin in the novel *Illusions perdues*. Later, in *Splendeurs et misères des courtisans,* he falls in love with a courtesan and after a series of unhappy

episodes, commits suicide in a prison cell. *Illusions perdues* is dedicated to Victor Hugo and is the occasion for an attack by Balzac on the dishonest Parisian press. *Illusions perdues* (Paris: Houssiaux, 1855): 1.

8. Quoted in César Graña, *Bohemian versus Bourgeois* (New York: Basic Books, 1964): 130. The author quotes Valery's description of Stendhal as a man for whom life was a private stage upon which he presented without interruption the performance of himself (p. 142).

9. *The World of Modern Fiction,* ed. Steven Marcus (New York: Simon & Schuster, 1966), vol. 1: xiii. However Joyce's notion applies to the Fry episode, Wouk in his work journal noted that *Youngblood Hawke* is "a full-scale Victorian novel, perhaps the first real one on the *far side of Joyce*" (emphasis supplied). Fry is obviously an important creation to Wouk. In a work journal note he describes Fry as "a great dividend of the book, a Greek chorus who does much to give it depth, and an important part of the dramatic situation."

10. Henry James, *The Art of the Novel: Critical Prefaces* (New York: Scribner's, 1962): 78.

11. "Leyte Gulf" was the working title of *Winds of War.* Wouk's determination is expressed in another journal entry: "I must execute this book to qualify for the execution of three bigger tasks ahead." This was Wouk's first novel in which the main character "ends tragically." In his next novel, *Don't Stop the Carnival,* one of the main characters, Iris Tramm, "ends tragically."

12. He is dismissive about *Slattery's Hurricane,* which he wrote as a screen treatment for 20th Century-Fox in 1948—"competence without truth."

13. Wouk's concern about Jewishness, understandable after the attacks on *Marjorie Morningstar* by Jewish critics, is seen in an entry dealing with an important subplot concerning the lease of a Kentucky coal mine by the mother of Youngblood Hawke—"I've been choking on it—this subplot—right along. The reason is that here without question I venture into new utterly gentile territory, and I greatly fear *Slattery's Hurricane*."

8

A Writer and His Ideas

Wouk is author of a number of other works published well before his two major novels about World War II. In this chapter I will discuss his play *The Traitor* (1949), his science fiction novella *The "Lomokome" Papers* (1949), his credo *This Is My God* (1959), and his moving introduction to a collection of letters by an Israeli war hero killed at Entebbe and published posthumously in 1980. The object of this discussion is to see what these works and others discussed earlier tell us about the novelist, his *idées maîtresses,* his values; in short, his "belief system."[1]

THE TRAITOR *COMES TO BROADWAY*

A two-act play, *The Traitor,* opened at the Forty-Eighth Street Theatre 31 March 1949 to generally good reviews.[2] The title figure, Professor Allen Carr, is a brilliant atomic scientist with no particular attachment to Marxism or Moscow but enslaved by the idea that he alone can save the world from atomic war. The best way to save the world from atomic war, he sincerely believes, is for the United States to hand over to the Soviet Union the secret of the atomic bomb which the Kremlin presumably lacked at the time.[3] Once both sides were in possession of the doomsday weapon, it would be in their mutual interest not to use it and to avoid the legendary fate of the two scorpions in the bottle.

However, U.S. intelligence officers, already suspicious of Carr, catch him more or less in *flagrante delicto.* Confronted by the accusations and already beginning to waver about the course he has been pursuing, Carr agrees to help trap the Russian secret agent with whom he is about to meet for the first time. The play ends with a shootout—the Soviet agent shoots Carr and the intelligence officers shoot the Soviet agent.

What is rather startling about the drama is that it was written well before the unmasking of Klaus Fuchs, the Rosenbergs, and the ambiguous politics of J. Robert Oppenheimer. There had been exposés of Soviet atomic espionage in Canada thanks to the defection of Igor Gouzenko, a Soviet attaché at the embassy in Ottawa in 1946. The scientist as traitor was something, however, quite new.

The play contains sociopolitical views which can be attributed to the author. For example, a subsidiary theme is whether Professor Tobias Emanuel, Carr's former philosophy teacher, should sign a loyalty questionnaire demanded of the faculty by the university president. Having been informed by the intelligence officers that Carr was probably guilty of espionage for the Russians, Emanuel decides to sign the paper because, as he tells Carr: "I believe it's right to force Communists out of their faculty posts."

Later when he tells a naval intelligence officer that he plans to sign the loyalty questionnaire, the young man, Lieutenant Henderson, tries to persuade him not to do so on the grounds that the Commuists have "a right to live their lives like anybody else, unless they commit a crime, and to hold their ideas." To which Emanuel replies that "I've felt exactly the way you do all my life. . . . These questionnaires at best are like fever therapy—infecting ourselves with one illness to cure another. But it now seems a serious public danger to me to allow Communists in the guise of educators to recruit among the immature for their secret work." And as he exits, Emanuel adds, "It's refreshing to find myself politically to the right of a Naval Intelligence officer."[4]

In an earlier dialogue with Carr, Professor Emanuel asks the physicist why he decided to help the Russians. Carr replies that he believed that if Russia acquired the bomb, the ensuing peace conference between the two superpowers would bring about "a real world government." Emanuel chides him about such certainty: "They're nations, led by men, haunted by illogical impulses of anger, suspicion, envy, and fear," and "the bomb in Russia's hands simply doubles the chance of an outbreak of atomic war." When Carr says that he was confronted by a conflict of loyalties—to his country or to all mankind—Emanuel replies: "Your mistake was contempt for the people and that's the Communists' mistake. They think the common man's too dumb to vote himself a just society. It has to be imposed on him by the clever few."

When Carr scoffs at the visible incapacities of the United States to deal intelligently with vital issues, Emanuel replies: "You see the flaw—and you miss the diamond. Our democratic process . . . has changed a wilderness into the happiest, strongest, most powerful nation of all history." Apparently, the argument with Emanuel persuades Carr, until that moment an arrogant, overbearing, and self-appointed spokesman for humankind, that he has been wrong. Emanuel then poses the alternatives: "Stand your ground as a traitor, Allen, because you believe in what you did—or work with Gallagher [the intelligence commander] because it's your duty as an American."

Despite a surface datedness, the play still reads well because the issues Wouk raised are still with us today—the sense of patriotism, the achievements of American democracy, the arrogance of the alienated intellectual embodied in Carr (shades of Keefer and Airman) who would live by his own ethical code. The voice of Wouk is that of Emanuel whose views of socialism and communism are fully congruent with Wouk's views then and now, specifically that Marxist doctrine has become a religion, "a faith without a God or a hereafter."[5]

THE "LOMOKOME" PAPERS

In writing the novella, Wouk's single effort at science fiction, the author intended to create "a mirror satire of nuclear confrontation." His 1949 "voyage to the moon" combines, he says in his preface to the new edition of 1968, three elements—romantic adventure, social satire, and a utopian sermon. (It seems a little short on the first ingredient.) He wrote the book, he says, while reading *Erewhon* and under the spell of Samuel Butler ("that prince of English prose") and Jonathan Swift's *A Modest Proposal.*[6]

The theme of the allegory, which science fiction frequently turns out to be, is simple: how to prevent the dwellers of the moon, divided into two hostile races, from destroying themselves by the use of a doomsday weapon, in this case "the silicon reaction." All this and more is written down in 107 scattered pages in the form of a journal recorded by Lieutenant Daniel More Butler, USN, lost on the moon. An astronaut, like Butler, who is sent to look for him finds only the remnants of the journal.[7]

The people of Lomokome (a Hebrew phrase meaning "no place," as the author explains) are constantly at war with the people of Lomadine (which in Hebrew could mean "no country," but the author does not say) "and the end of days is at hand." Lieutenant Butler comes across "The Book of Ctuzelawis," written by the son of a union rare on the moon—the marriage between a Lomadine woman and a Lomokome metallurgist. The name they give their only son means in moon language "Would-that-wars-would-cease."

This piece of science fiction was set in 1948-49, before U.S.-Soviet negotiations had even been contemplated, before even the hydrogen bomb had been built. Some of Wouk's ideas may seem rather dated, but it was not bad forecasting for the 1970s and 1980s. "The Book of Ctuzelawis" argues that treaties will not work, negotiations to destroy the ultimate "silicon reaction" weapons, or the idea of world government will not work because "nobody wants it." Says the moon prophet: "War is no evil. We love to say it is, but we do not believe it. War is necessary to us. You need war as you need food."

The only solution is to control war under the Law of Reasonable War. A College of Judges is to be set up with equal representation from Lomokome and Lomadine. These will be the wisest of mankind and upon appointment will cease to be citizens of either moon country. It will be their job when war is declared to measure the war effort and after comparing the effort of both sides to award the victory.

Without some deaths in battle, Reasonable War might become too popular and lead to perpetual war. So at the end of a war, the College of Judges will calculate the number of people to die on each side in proportion to the general verdict of victory and defeat. Each government will thereupon kill the required number of their own people on what will be observed as Death Day.

At the outbreak of war, death offices will be opened in both countries to enlist volunteers to die upon the verdict of the College of Judges. The final selection will be by lot. The College of Judges will also determine how many older people will die.

The moon prophet points to the advantage of his proposal: "You will be able to fight each other to the end of time. You will have the delights and stimulation of everlasting enmity. But the sorrow of war will be kept within decorous bounds. You will prosper, for you will continually be busy. . . . You will live in quiet and safety. The damage that war can do will be bounded, not boundless as in the old days. . . . Death in war you will have. But it will be a reasonable slaughter."

What Wouk has done here is defy in one sense the conventions of science fiction which, says Brian W. Aldiss, hangs on an optimism about human nature. Most science fiction suffers from "the fatal error . . . that revolution, or a new gimmick, or a bunch of strong men, or an invasion of aliens, or the conquest of other planets, or the annihilation of half the world—in short, pretty nearly anything but the facing up to the integral and irredeemable nature of mankind—can bring about a utopian situation. It is the old error of the externalization of evil."[8] Wouk has offered us a vision of a Hobbesian world whose survival depends not on trying to alter the unalterable—human nature—but rather on making the unreasonable appear reasonable.

THIS IS MY GOD

Wouk's book about the meaning of Judaism is intertwined with his religious orthodoxy, his faith in Zionism and the State of Israel, and a firmly held belief that Jewish history, despite its many episodic tragedies like the Nazi Holocaust, is not meaningless.[9] The book's title is based on a line from the Song of Moses (Exodus 15:2): "This my God and I will praise him; The God of my fathers and will exalt him."[10] Like all testaments of faith, Wouk's words are unarguable except for those readers, critics, religious leaders who interpret differently the same liturgics, the same ceremonies and observances, the same biblical passage.

The volume is the story of a spiritual pilgrimage as well as an exegetical text; everything you ever wanted to know about Judaism but did not know what to ask. The spiritual pilgrimage is necessarily autobiographical in part; no one can write a personal confession of faith without it assuming the shape of an autobiography.[11] The book is dedicated to his grandfather and inductor into Judaism, Mendel Leib Levine, who was an important influence on Wouk as I have indicated earlier. The book became an immediate nonfiction best-seller. The profits, says Wouk in an introduction, have gone to a fund for charity and education established by himself and his wife in 1954, "in memory of our first-born son, Abe."[12]

In his dedication, Wouk discusses his awareness "of the deep lacks" of his book, that the theme "needs a prophet," that the subject demands "monumental scholarship." As his own apologia he cites a maxim from one of the basic texts of Judaic lore, *The Ethics of the Fathers:* "The work is not yours to finish; but neither are you free to take no part in it."

The work is divided into five parts, the fifth being an afterword written for the reissued edition. The titles of the first four are self-explanatory—"The Remarkable Survival of the Jews"; "The Faith"; "The Law"; "The Present." It answers questions like: "How true is all this?"—meaning the Bible; the core of Judaism; popularity of Yom Kippur; the problem of prayer; must prayer be in Hebrew? where does authority lie? what the Talmud is like; who is Orthodox?

SELF-PORTRAIT OF A HERO

Wouk's introduction to this volume of letters demonstrates with even greater clarity than anything he has written before the tremendous meaning of the return of the Jews to Israel after nineteen centuries of exile; the spiritual significance to everything he believes in of this return, and his admiration for the soldiers, like Netanyahu. Even though Netanyahu "was respectful of our religion," he was not an observing Jew.[13] Yet Wouk did something quite unusual for him. Usually his day starts with a reading of Scripture or Talmud study. When the Netanyahu letters came to him, then in Hebrew (among religious Jews the language is referred to as *lushen ha'kodesh,* the holy language), he began his day by reading them instead.

His admiration for the soldier's military prowess leads him to a comparison of the Israeli with one of Wouk's heroes, Admiral Raymond Spruance, the U.S. naval commander who led and won the Battle of Midway against what appeared almost hopeless odds. The World War II naval hero and the Israeli are for Wouk the kind of men "who embody—by the cast of destiny—the virtue of their whole people in a great hour." Spruance is an important figure in Wouk's *War and Remembrance.*

In this introduction as in *This Is My God,* Wouk demonstrates a love of America rare in modern American literature. The book of letters of the fallen Yoni Netanyahu is for American fighters, "to reassure them that their love of country is noble, that self-sacrifice is rewarding, that to be ready to fight for freedom fills a man with a sense of worth like nothing else."[14]

> If the United States of America is not another preposterous historical anomaly—the last gasp on earth of the dream of freedom, in a world collapsing into authoritarianism or benighted chaos; if America is still the great beacon in dense gloom, the promise to the hundreds of millions of the oppressed that liberty exists, that it is the shining future, that they can throw off their tyrants, and learn freedom and cease learning war— then we, too, like Israel, need our Yonis to stand guard in the night.

WOUK'S BELIEF SYSTEM

There is a strong internal consistency to the author's belief system, rooted in Orthodox Judaism. This faith explains a great deal about his views on sexual morality, the outgrowth of fidelity to tradition and ethics.[15] He is strongly against the Soviet Union as a totalitarian dictatorship and as an enemy of the Jewish people within the Soviet Union. He is opposed to Marxist socialism although he believes profoundly in social justice. And he believes most strongly that Americanism and Judaism are compatible.[16]

The key to Wouk's belief system is not just his Judaism but his veneration of Orthodox Judaism rather than either of the two off-shoots, Conservative or Reform Judaism. His Judaism and way of life are a veneration of tradition as against modern scientism, which denies the truth and validity of "traditional and institutional life and a refusal to accept authority on any grounds except those of scientific principles."[17] From this belief system comes his commitment to the traditional novel with its faith in the normal life.

NOTES

1. "A belief system is defined as a relation between attitudes, such that if we knew a person's attitude to one set of issues we would have some success in predicting his attitudes to others." Samuel Brittan, *Left or Right: The Bogus Dilemma* (London: Secker & Warburg, 1968):45
2. *The Traitor,* which ran for less than a month, seemed doomed from the start despite a strong cast, e.g., Lee Tracy and Walter Hampden, and staging by the capable Jed Harris. However, it opened during Lent in 1949, a bad time for Broadway productions; a general taxi strike began on opening night; there was little advance publicity and no out-of-town tryout and almost no advance sale.
3. The first Soviet atomic test came in August 1949 and was followed by the arrest and confession of Klaus Fuchs, a top-ranking British nuclear physicist who had been spying for the Russians. Fuchs was convicted in March 1950. Atomic espionage did not figure in the Alger Hiss case where a Grand Jury indictment was handed down in December 1948. Nor did the 6 March 1949 arrest of Judith Coplon have to do with atomic espionage. David Caute, *The Great Fear: The Anti-Communist Purge under Truman and Eisenhower* (New York: Simon & Schuster, 1978):61, 63, 466, passim.
4. The loyalty questionnaire is the occasion of another speech by the intelligence commander, Captain Gallagher, who tells Carr that by his actions "the words science and scientist are going to stink all over America. . . . You think the questionnaires are an insult to your profession? You've vindicated them all. From now on scientists are going to get a Spanish Inquisition with modern trimmings. And us military mossbacks, us Pentagon lowbrows, will have to apply the thumb screws, as usual."
5. "Marxism is not simply an economic doctrine; it is a doctrine about the universe, and such doctrines are held with religious rather than with scientific attitudes. . . . For it is a feature of religious thinking that it should inevitably make cosmological claims of some sort. But more important in relation to the religious aspect is the emergence of a conception of doctrinal orthodoxy within Marxism." Alasdair C. MacIntyre, *Marxism: An Interpretation* (London: SCM, 1953):101.
6. The full title of Swift's satire (1729) is *A Modest Proposal for Preventing the Children of Poor People from Being a Burden to Their Parents or the Country.* Swift's solution was for the rich to eat the children. The chapter on musical banks in *Erewhon* (Butler's anagram for "nowhere") was drawn on by Wouk as a satire on churchly institutions. Other influences cited by the author include Marjorie Nicolson's *Voyages to the Moon* and

First Men on the Moon by H. G. Wells, regarded as the father of modern science fiction.

7. The naval lieutenant's middle name is derived from Sir Thomas More, author of *Utopia,* and the last name, of course, from Samuel Butler.

8. In *The Mirror of Infinity,* ed. Robert Silverberg (New York: Harper & Row, 1970):287. Aldiss, quite properly, is regarded as one of the major figures in British science fiction. The book itself is an anthology of science fiction chosen by critics like Aldiss, Robert Conquest, Kingsley Amis, and others, with short introductory essays attached to each of the thirteen stories.

9. This is Wouk's invocation: "As for me, I declare my faith that our history is not meaningless and that nihilism is a hallucination of sick men. God lives, and we are his people, chosen to live by his name and his law until the day when the Lord will be one and his name one. We are nothing at all, or we are a people apart, marked by history for a fate embracing the heights and depths of the human experience. We live; and we live in a time when we can draw breath in freedom and renew our starved-out strength." In *This Is My God* (New York: Pocket Books, 1974):237. I am using the paperback edition because it has been revised and contains an afterword dealing with the Six-Day War.

10. The King James version has a somewhat different version of the lines which are an epigraph in Wouk's book. The passage is also different in the Alexander Harkavy translation of 1916 (New York: Hebrew Publishing), vol. 2:113. The English version reads: "The Lord is my strength and song, and he is become my salvation; he is my God, and I will adorn him; my father's God and I will exalt him."

11. *Apologia pro Vita Sua* by Cardinal Newman (New York: Dutton, 1912) is a good example. What started as an explanation and refutation of Charles Kingsley's polemics against Newman became a detailed history of Newman's credo and how he got there.

12. Wouk refers to the death of his first-born son in the introduction to *Self-Portrait of a Hero: The Letters of Jonathan Netanyahu* (New York: Random House, 1980):vi: "My wife and I lost Abe in a tragic and senseless accident, a month or so before his fifth birthday."

13. Ibid., p. vii. The distinction between "respect" for Judaism and religious observance is quite common among Jews.

14. Wouk was writing this preface at the time when the Khomeini regime had seized the American hostages and the Entebbe-like attempt to rescue them had failed.

15. See pp. 124ff. of *This Is My God,* which deals with marriage, adultery, and sex. It is difficult to see how Wouk feels about the woman's liberation movement. In discussing sex, for example, he says that while in other cultures intercourse "has been a deed of shame, or of comedy, or of orgy, or of physical necessity, or high romance," in Judaism it is "one of the main things God wants *men* to do" (emphasis added). Quite probably the Old Testament does not credit women with sex instincts or desires which need God's urging. As for homosexuality, since Scriptures ban that practice, it finds no tolerance in Wouk.

16. Wouk's attitude toward the Soviet Union is colored by the dictatorship's rigorous anti-Semitic policies. In *This Is My God* (p. 76), he writes: "Our

religion the Soviets consider a barbarous relic, superseded in wisdom and soundness by Marxism. The training of children in this exploded Semitic superstition goes against good sense and the interests of the state. So the police discourage such teaching, in ways sometimes oblique and sometimes forcible." In a commencement address at Yeshiva College (23 June 1953, mimeo) he addressed himself to the liberal tradition, by whose timetable the millennium should have arrived with the fall of the czar and the kaiser. "What arrived instead . . . was the year of Lenin and his three pupils, Mussolini, Stalin, and Hitler. . . . All three won men's hearts and minds through the magic of one and the same idea—socialism. . . . We see now that for all the shades of ideology, for all the clouds of words, Lenin, Stalin, Hitler, and Mussolini were always essentially alike, that they were the Caligulas, the Neroes, the Borgias of the twentieth century, and that they almost destroyed the liberal tradition while crying each in his own evil accents about social justice." The liberals, he said, were too forgiving of the Russian Marxists (p. 2).
17. Edward Shils in *The Radical Left,* ed. Geberding and Smith (Boston: Houghton Mifflin, 1971):121

9

The Greatness: The War Novels

"In the fifth century storm upon storm out of the dark North swept away in a great deluge of barbarism all the civilization of the western half of the Roman Empire." So, portentously, begins G. F. Young's history of the Medici.[1] The sentence could well describe the first half of the twentieth century with its two world wars, the holocaust of peoples and particularly European Jewry, the era of revolutionary tyrannies—an unprecedented deluge of barbarism which, as one looks at Poland, Afghanistan, Southeast Asia, Central America, the Middle East, has not ended yet.

It is to this catastrophic era, its essence concentrated in the years between 1939 and 1945, that Wouk turned his artistic vision and sense of history and began composing his two war novels—*Winds of War* and *War and Remembrance*. Together the novels total more than 1,900 pages and one million words. He began the first novel in July 1965, just after publication of *Youngblood Hawke,* and completed the second in July 1978, thirteen years of extraordinary research and long, arduous composition.

The novels were enormously successful with reading publics. From the sales figures alone, it can be said that more people in America and elsewhere have learned about World War II from Wouk than from any other novelist or historian. The only major reading public barred from access to Wouk is the Soviet, where Wouk is regarded as a nonauthor. This Soviet decision may account for Wouk's enormous popularity in the People's Republic of China, where *Winds of War* and *War and Remembrance* have, since 1980, sold a million copies. Such sales make Wouk the most widely published and distributed contemporary American writer in the PRC, according to an American Embassy report (10 November 1982) on the occasion of the visit of Wouk and his wife as guests of the Chinese Writers Association. (The report was made available to the writer 17 June 1983.) The second most widely printed

American work is Alex Haley's *Roots,* but the total sold is little more than 100,000. Other American writers who circulate in China in editions of the low thousands include Saul Bellow, John Cheever, Joseph Heller, Bernard Malamud, and Susan Sontag.

The American Embassy believes that Wouk's works were given unusual attention for several reasons, some cultural, some political: 1. Chinese readers enjoy long novels, e.g., *Dream of the Red Chamber;* 2. World War II is a period of special interest to the Chinese; 3. Wouk writes with special authority about naval warfare, something of interest to China, possessing a navy for the first time since the early Ming dynasty; 4. Despite the PRC's anti-Israeli stand, Chinese are strongly interested in the Holocaust and other aspects of the Jewish experience; 5. The government's desire to correct a 1980 Chinese-written World War II history which followed the Soviet line completely on all aspects of the war.[2] Another reason, unmentioned in the embassy report, is the ancient maxim: "The enemy of my enemy is my friend." If Wouk is a nonauthor in the Soviet Union he deserves recognition in China. The last reason may be that Wouk is a bonanza for the Chinese government. No royalties are paid him for his novels, which have been distributed on a scale unprecedented for the literary work of a foreigner. China can pirate what it pleases since it does not adhere to the international copyright convention.

To a critic who has had unrestricted access to Wouk's papers, the boxes of uncatalogued materials about these two novels was a treasure-trove—pages of research, interviews with military experts, participant-observers, naval officers of high and low rank, historians, Holocaust victims, first-person memoranda of historical events, on-the-spot research in faraway places where battles blazed and war lords negotiated the uneasy peace. It is rare to find so much raw material about the makings of a modern war novel.

ANOMALOUS LITERARY GENRE

The genre of the historical novel is an anomalous literary creation. Its existence begins, perhaps, with Daniel Defoe or Sir Walter Scott.[3] For a writer, the problems in fashioning a historical novel are enormous. The plot, it must be assumed, is known to the reader; there can be no surprises or unexpected twists because the plot is preordained by history. An author can play games by adopting a "what if" approach— what if Lincoln had lived—but then the author has moved into an entirely different genre, fantasy, since history does not offer alternatives. The anomalousness of the historical novel consists in that it brazenly exploits historical characters and events known to all, mixes them with what Georg Lukács called "middling" figures[4] who never existed, lovingly involving them with the universals of narrative literature to produce a masterpiece, say, like Tolstoy's *War and Peace.*

For Wouk, the Defoe *Memoirs of a Cavalier* had a large influence on the structure of his novels about the war. In his journal on *Winds of War* he notes that Winston Churchill in both his great war histories cited Defoe's *Memoirs* as his model for historical narrative strung on the adventures of one person. As Wouk says: "This novel follows the identical model. It is closer to the method of Defoe in that the protagonist is an imaginary figure and not, as in the Churchill works, the author himself, a leading figure in both wars. My cavalier is Victor Henry. The narrative pursues the adventures of his family as well as himself."[5] Victor Henry, nicknamed Pug, is the central character of both war novels. He is a navy career officer and when *Winds of War* opens he is forty-nine, married, and father of three children.

The vast, panoramic, minutely detailed historical or epic novel has been thoroughly repudiated by some critics and contemporary novelists. For example, Mary McCarthy has warned about "the fetishism of fact" among novelists. She singles out Herman Melville because of his insistence in *Moby Dick* on telling the reader everything to be known about whaling; Dostoyevsky who, in *The Brothers Karamazov,* has a long disquisition about the history of the role of the elder in Russian monasticism; Tolstoy who, in *War and Peace,* recounts the history of Freemasonry because Pierre Bezuhov becomes interested in that institution; Thomas Mann and the long passages on tuberculosis in *The Magic Mountain;* and Balzac's chapter in *Illusions perdues* on how paper is made, inserted in the book because the hero has inherited a paper factory.[6]

McCarthy Misses the Point

McCarthy ignores the need for backdrop, for foreground, and peripheral detail in a novel, particularly in a historical romance where the writer is not only creating but also recreating. It would be like criticizing the superb military painter Emile Jean-Horace Vernet for the enormous detail in his sweeping canvas *The Battle of Montmirail.* Hilaire Belloc once wrote: "A man may be ever so accurately informed as to the dates, the hours, the weather, the gestures, the type of speech, the very words, the soil, the colour, that between them all would seem to build up a particular event. But if he is not seized of the mind which lay behind all that was human in the business, then no synthesis of his detailed knowledge is possible."[7]

It is quite clear from a careful study of Wouk's war novels that he has not only accurately informed himself about the actual events between 1939 and 1945 to a degree which has evoked praise from professional historians, but that he was "seized of the mind which lay behind all that was human in the business."[8]

An Exercise in Futility

To summarize the two war novels in a few pages would be an exercise in futility since, in one sense, one would be narrating the history of World War II and its cast of characters who made or contributed to that history—Roosevelt, Churchill, Stalin, Hitler, Mussolini, Goering, Harry Hopkins, the generals, admirals, submariners, aviators, and the Auschwitz camp commandant and the killing machine over which he presided. There are subplots galore, dozens of them—the willful obtuseness of the U.S. Department of State which refused to believe the documented terrors of the Holocaust while millions burned; the overpowering narrative of the Battle of Midway and then Leyte Gulf and the men who died in those battles; the extraordinary Potemkin scenes at the Nazi murder camp of Theriesenstadt. It is there that death stalks Aaron Jastrow, one of the most memorable personalities in modern fiction, a Jewish immigrant to America, a writer, a philosopher, an apostate who in the last days of his life returns to his early faith with a sermon, secretly delivered to his camp fellows, on the meaning of Job.

War and Remembrance is really seven novels in one. It is the story of the war in the Pacific and the submarine war. It is a novel about the Nazi invasion of Russia and about the siege of Leningrad and Stalingrad. It is about Washington in wartime, the birth of the atomic bomb, about human frailties, love affairs, marriages, divorces, the death of loved ones. It contains the extraordinary memoirs of a fictive German general and how he viewed the war and Hitler. And, of course, the Holocaust. Perhaps there is an eighth theme—Wouk's love and veneration of the U.S. Navy and his almost worshipful portrait of Admiral Raymond A. Spruance, who made history at Midway in 1942.

No Confusing Anarchy

Despite the plots, subplots, criss-crossing narratives, and beginnings and endings, a master novelist is at the helm and the authenticity is never marred by confusing anarchy. There is in these two books a demonstration of Wouk's great forte, a sense of narrative unity—which has been attributed to George Eliot and her Victorian novel *Middle-*

march—the genius with which a novelist connects the various plots of a novel and the fusion of many concurrent stories and "of constantly switching the reader's attention from one character or set of charcters to another." It is the ability to control the inevitable proliferation of event and character in a novel whose setting is, literally, the entire world.[9]

What makes Wouk's two novels unique in World War II literature is that he takes the war seriously, in old-fashioned terms, as *war,* as something which was worth fighting, which it was imperative to fight. For him war, and particularly World War II, is not a convenient metaphor symbolizing the twentieth-century plight of mankind or some kind of cuckoo's nest in which there are no heroes but only madmen, villains, sadists, or lecherous GIs. He hates war and yet realizes, as Reinhold Niebuhr once said, "Tyranny is worse than war."[10]

SERIOUS RESEARCH ABOUT WORLD WAR II

The seriousness with which Wouk has dealt with the war can be seen in the prodigious amount of research, reading, travel, and conferring with experts, the evidence for which is to be found in the uncataloged boxes at Columbia University. It is not merely the hundreds and hundreds of books he read about the war, the films and newsreels about the war which he rented and screened, and the long interviews with men like Vice-Admiral John L. McCrea, who had been FDR's naval aide during the war. What is striking about his research is the humility with which he approached the scholars whose help he enlisted.

Most interesting and illustrative of Wouk's temperament is his correspondence with the late Professor Walter Kaufmann of Princeton, a distinguished philosopher grounded in German history, philosophy, and culture. It was from Kaufmann that Wouk received a trenchant critique about the memoirs of the fictive German general Armin von Roon, titled *World Empire Lost,* an invention from start to finish but one which, as a literary device, is brilliant in aim and achievment.

The Princeton adviser analyzed the German general's memoir in highly critical language including von Roon's original name, Wolfgang von Goethe, which, said Kaufmann, is "like having a British general called William Shakespeare or an American general, Abraham Lincoln." The letter, dated 17 June 1970, led to a Princeton meeting between Wouk and Kaufmann on 14 July, which lasted five and a half hours during which both men reviewed Kaufmann's analysis page by page. Kaufmann singled out for special criticism Wouk's discussion, via the German general, of the philosophical and cultural sources of Nazism.

The same archive includes the draft of a letter which was never sent to Kaufmann and in which Wouk describes his meeting as "a bruising business, but no other kind would have been worth a long trip and five and a half intensive hours." He tells Kaufmann that "you have made a serious contribution to the editing process on this challenging task. You took the job seriously and kindly mixed candor and tact, and on your specialty—German culture and its relationship to Nazism—you made the clarifying attack which more than anything I looked for from you." It is not clear in this file what letter, if any, Wouk did send to Kaufmann.

Other experts whom Wouk consulted and from whom he solicited advice and comments included Howard K. Smith, the news broadcaster, Harrison Salisbury, Llewellyn Thompson, U.S. diplomat and Soviet specialist, Admiral Lewis L. Strauss, onetime head of the Atomic Energy Commission, and Air Vice-Marshal Crowley-Milling. Of particular help was Raul Hilberg, author of *The Destruction of The European Jews*. Hilberg, then a professor at the University of Vermont, considered von Roon, the German general, "one of the most powerful characters in the novel. Though all but unseen his whole personality comes through as he writes his thoughts about the war. He is a compelling man, complex and yet utterly sure of himself, but I think he could be made stronger still."[11]

IN THE PENUMBRA

The problem for a historical novelist is not only that all his historical characters, as suggested earlier, come ready made, but also that even the middling characters have trouble growing with the narrative. They often seem doomed to live within the penumbra of the world-historic individuals.

It is Wouk's great achievement that he has created middling characters of a striking autonomy. One such powerful figure is Berel Jastrow, cousin of Aaron Jastrow. Aaron lives in a dream world of rationality as becomes a Yale history professor, a friend of the Archbishop of Siena and author of *A Jew's Jesus*. His cousin, Berel, knows better. He and his family are on the firing line as World War II begins with the invasion of Poland. We meet Berel when Natalie Jastrow, Aaron's niece, goes to visit Berel with her future husband, Byron Henry, in a town near Cracow.

BEREL, THE JOYCEAN GIANT

As the war spreads and the slaughter of the Polish Jews begins, Berel takes form. His is the eye of a man who is everywhere. For Wouk, Berel becomes someone like the dead giant who rises up in Joyce's *Finnegan's Wake,* a sort of superreal figure. It is Berel who brings out the first news of the Nazi slaughter of the Russian Jews in Minsk to an unbelieving audience in Washington, London, and in Nazi-occupied Europe.

In his work journal, Wouk plans the introduction of Berel, now a prisoner of the Wehrmacht and brought to the town of Oswiecim, renamed Auschwitz by the Nazis. Before the war's outbreak, Berel lived and worked in Auschwitz. For Wouk, Berel becomes the "Auschwitz Presence," through whom he will "recreate Auschwitz as a reality . . . as it was *experienced* . . . to open the shut hearts and minds, my own included, to relive and to remember." In Hebrew letters, Wouk writes the word *Zuchor,* remember. Berel is going to be a death camp survivor, a supremely clever man "who managed to make himself sufficiently useful to the Germans so that he hung on. In the meantime he did his best for the unfortunates around him, always short of getting killed himself." And, continues Wouk: "I have kept silent for twenty-five years while everybody else has had a pass at it. Now let us see if love of God, love of the Jews, grasp, penetration, and art can bring this thing to life and grief. Grief, the true drive wheel here, even more than ambition."

Berel, miraculously, wandered in and out of death camps, journeyed to Russia, through the Carpathians to Prague and finally met his end in a wood outside Prague; his bones lie unmarked, "like so many bones over Europe." Wouk ends his novel with these words:

> Berel Jastrow was never born and never existed. He was a parable. In truth his bones stretch from the French coast to the Urals, dry bones of a murdered giant. And in truth a marvelous thing happens; his story does not end there, for the bones stand up and take on flesh. God breathes spirit into the bones, and Berel Jastrow turns eastward and goes home.[12]

NOTES

1. G.F. Young, *The Medici* (New York: Modern Library, 1930): 1.
2. André Schiffrin, "Letter from China: Window on the West," *New York Times Book Review* (18 July 1982): 7. *Winds of War* was one of the first books to be translated after the Cultural Revolution ended, because, said a

Chinese Communist spokesman, it dealt with "the anti-Fascist war." However, Saul Bellow's novels are the most widely translated American works in China. Schiffrin was clearly disturbed by this news about the popularity of Wouk and Bellow in a communist country, since he regards these writers as informed by "conservative views." He would be hard put to explain why the great writers and poets of the century—Yeats, Faulkner, Eliot, D.H. Lawrence, Wyndham Lewis, Ezra Pound, Paul Claudel, Céline, Bernanos, and earlier Flaubert, Conrad, Tolstoy, Dostoyevsky—have been "more often than not skeptical or conservative or outrightly reactionary in relation to radical or revolutionary claims—in politics, if not in art." Eugene Goodheart, *Culture and the Radical Conscience* (Cambridge, Mass.: Harvard University Press, 1973): 84. See also J.R. Harrison, *The Reactionaries* (London: Gollancz, 1966). Engels thought that "Balzac, in spite of his reactionary opinions, was worth a thousand Zolas, though Zola's sympathies were strongly democratic." John Lehman, *New Writing in Europe* (London: Pelican, 1940): 150. Another interesting study is Grattan Freyer, *W.B. Yeats and the Anti-Democratic Tradition* (Dublin: Gill & Macmillan, 1982). None of this is intended to imply that Wouk and Bellow are reactionaries, but rather that life is not so simple as Schiffrin thinks.

3. Daniel Defoe's *Memoirs of a Cavalier* (1724) has all the attributes of a historical novel. However, the genre really came into its own with the historical romances of Sir Walter Scott. Avrom Fleishman, *The English Historical Novel: Walter Scott to Virginia Woolf* (Baltimore: Johns Hopkins University Press, 1971): 23ff.

4. Georg Lukács, *The Historical Novel* (London: Penguin, 1981): 37, 40, passim. Lukács makes the point that whereas the novelist always attempts to show the development of character, neither Scott nor any author of historical fiction can really show the evolution of great historical personalities, Hegel's "world-historical individuals." Instead, says Lukács, the author "always presents us with the personality complete" (p. 38).

5. The full titles of Defoe's novel is *Memoirs of a Cavalier or a Military Journal of the Wars in Germany and the Wars in Scotland from the Year 1632 to the Year 1648 Written about Four Score Years Ago by an English Gentleman Who First Served in the Army of Gustavus Adolphus, the Glorious King of Sweden till His Death and After That in the Royal Army of King Charles I from the Beginning of the Rebellion to the End of That War.* The novel has seventeen chapters totaling 231 pages. It is in a collection of *Novels and Miscellaneous Works* by Defoe, published in London by Henry Bone, 1854. See also William P. Trent, *Daniel Defoe: How to Know Him* (Indianapolis: Bobbs-Merrill, 1960): 173.

6. Mary McCarthy, "The Fact in Fiction," in *On the Contrary* (New York: Farrar, Straus & Cudahy, 1961): 258.

7. Hilaire Belloc, "On Knowing the Past," in *This and That and the Other* (London: Methuen, 1912): 229.

8. Henry Kissinger in a letter to the publishers (Little, Brown) of Wouk's *War And Remembrance* wrote: "His treatment of history is brilliant. He has more than recaptured the period: he has given it life and at the same time supplied enormous insight into the larger forces and ideas that were at work." Michael Mandelbaum says that the events in both volumes "are

described in scrupulous detail with impressive fidelity to the historical record. . . . Conventional histories of the war find it difficult to tie together these farflung theatres. Wouk successfully integrates them. . . . Wouk's two books give more vivid pictures of the principal leaders of the war than military and political history could. Fiction is better than history at showing 'how it really was' where matters of human character are concerned." "The Political Lessons of Two World War II Novels: A Review Essay," *Political Science Quarterly* 94 (Fall 1979): 515–22. Paul Fussell wrote a particularly perverse review of *War and Remembrance* as a novel but praised Wouk's "scholarship in contemporary history," his "role of naval historian," as good as Samuel Eliot Morison, and who as a narrator of land battle "invites comparison with someone like B.H. Liddell Hart." Wouk's description of "significant public environments and 'things' " are "wonderful." Says Fussell: "There's hardly a contemporary writer so good at depicting locales authentically. . . . They are perfect." *New Republic* (14 October 1978).

9. W.J. Harvey, introduction to George Eliot, *Middlemarch* (London: Penguin, 1965): 9, 12.

10. Quoted in Jacob van Rossum, "Reinhold Niebuhr's Case against Pacifism," *This World* (Summer 1982): 25. In an essay titled "Why the Church Is Not Pacifist," he wrote in 1940: "Whatever may be the moral ambiguities of the so-called democratic nations . . . it is sheer moral perversity to equate the inconsistencies of a democratic civilization with the brutalities which modern tyrannical states practise. If we cannot make a distinction here, there are no historical distinctions which have any value." Ibid., p. 20.

11. Mandelbaum (p. 517) says "a special invention of the two novels brings home the scope of the war with particular force"—the von Roon memoirs which are "based on actual postwar writings of German officers. For Roon, the war's global dimension offered opportunities that could have changed history." Von Roon wrote these memoirs in a prison cell. For complicity in war crimes on the eastern front, he received a 20-year sentence at the Nuremberg trials.

12. A lot of the source material of *War and Remembrance* is in box 16 of the Wouk collection at Columbia University.

10

Looking Forward: A Nonconclusion

A critical yet sympathetic and admiring reader (and in my special case, a careful rereader) comes to a simple conclusion: Wouk gets better and better as he ages. His technical virtuosity keeps pace with his creativity and artistic ambition. His will to swim against the tide of modern novelistic convention, as concretized by *Ulysses*, the novel to end novels, grows stronger. Like that of Samuel Richardson, whom he so admires, Wouk's aim is not only to entertain but also, as a novelist involved with society, to fix basic moral issues upon the collective conscience of free men.

Wouk is one of the few novelists concerned with virtue, a recurrent theme in his novels and plays. For him, man's fate is meaningful, not a random, capricious happening. Like few other novelists, he realizes that man does not live by psychological motivation alone. The Freudian-Marxist age which sits heavily on our literary culture holds no attraction for Wouk. Final answers are hard to come by even with prayer and devotion. And surely final answers are not to be found lying on a couch or peering over a barricade.

RELIGIOUS VALUES

As a novelist, Wouk argues that values are not to be overcome by the spontaneity of *chacun à son goût*, but rather that values are permanent and enduring, especially when they come out of religion rather than culture. There is little that is obscurantist or enigmatic in his behavior as artist and literary strategist. For Wouk, the real world is illuminated by imagination intensified by indomitable faith and divine spirit. For him, literature means a continuing scrutiny of mankind's prospects as seen through the eyes of the warrior, statesman, solipsist intellectual, philosopher, apostate, the poet *maudit*, wandering giant, the faithless and the faithful, the misanthrope killer god and his demonic Auschwitzians, the martyred, and finally, the dry bones in the valley that await redemption.

They all speak through this writer for whom literature is part of the darkening history of a civilization approaching an Ozymandian finality. It is strange to think that the key to Wouk's career as an artist, as he himself has said, is *Don Quixote.* When he first read it in 1944, "a whole world opened to me and I suddenly realized what the novel really was." Said Wouk:

> I write a traditional novel, which is rather unfashionable, and I've taken a lot of kicking for it. The critics may be right, and yet in my judgment the classic novel . . . is alive and we're experiencing the end of the experimental period, and that the classic novel will come back very strongly. Whether my books will live is another question entirely. But the strength of my work comes from this intense grounding in the 18th and 19th century novelists [Tolstoy, Dickens, Sterne, Trollope, Richardson].[1]

CRITICISM OF THE WAR NOVELS

It is quite true that Wouk has been savaged by some critics, patronized by others, and ignored by still others. Yet there has been a macabrely amusing side to these onslaughts. In exaggerated polemical fashion, Christopher Lehmann-Haupt, the *New York Times* book critic, tears into *War and Remembrance* with a blind rage—the accusation that Wouk fudges moral issues, for example, reveals more about the critic's wrong-headedness than about Wouk's ethical sense—and then praises the book as "splendidly entertaining" and for depicting historic events in a fashion that is "sometimes downright awesome." Mind you, here is a book of more than 1,000 pages not of entertainment—how the *Times* critic can call the novel "splendidly entertaining" when one recalls the graphic, horrifying descriptions of Auschwitz and the presence of Adolf Eichmann is beyond me—but rather of a world drowning in ethical crises—Hiroshima, Dresden, death camps, self-sacrificing submarine captains—and Mr. Lehmann-Haupt can end his review with a real fudge: "Don't think about 'War and Remembrance' too much and you'll have a wonderful time."[2] Jolly old Theriesenstadt!

The review by Pearl K. Bell, while gentler in tone than Lehmann-Haupt's, was full of scorn and contempt—the novel never "rises above the sentimental level of best-selling romance"; Wouk is trapped by "the stale and debilitating conventions of popular fiction"; "the sentimentality that blights his fictional episodes"; "the fictional creatures playing out his romance seem not merely trivial but offensively so." Despite the "soap-opera crudities" of *Winds of War*, Bell says, "I could not, as the saying goes, put [it] down." But for *War and Remembrance*? "For one thing, its burdensome thousand-page bulk is a lot harder to pick up than to put down." I have heard it said that one should not judge a book by its cover; in the light of Bell's criticism, that statement must now be amended: one should not judge a book by its weight or number of pages.

Bell, one of our more perceptive and enlightened critics, sees Wouk's uniqueness as a novelist, namely, that he is "in unabashed dissent from the main-stream of American novelists today, for whom the only credible hero is the anti-hero"; that "he remains an unembarrassed believer in such 'discredited' forms of commitment as valor, gallantry, leadership, patriotism." Wouk's "unfashionable convictions will predictably strike many reviewers . . . as at best naive, at worst absurdly out of touch with the Catch-22 lunacy of all war, including the war against Hitler." She praises Wouk for his "brilliant simulation of the Nazi military mind [by] an ingenious device"—the memoirs of the imaginary German general, von Roon. She finds it "impossible to deny the dignity and decency that inform Wouk's sense of . . . moral obligation, which sustained his prodigious effort of research and writing between 1962 and 1978." Still the novel cannot be judged "by any valid standard [as] a successfully realized work of literature."[3]

WHAT "VALID STANDARD"?
•

At a time when there is a wide and spreading recognition that the dominant and mainstream literary culture in this country opposes standards; when the counterculture has so strengthened the philistine demiurge as to ensure the early fulfillment of Richard Hofstadter's prophecy a decade ago that the years through which we have lived would be known to later historians as "The Age of Rubbish," one can only ask: what "valid standard" is Bell talking about? Is there today any standard left other than that which emerges out of one's conscience and one's sense of humanity and decency?

What "valid standard" did Anthony Burgess incorporate in his letter to Wouk (20 May 1980) about the war novels when he wrote that "the whole work . . . is of Tolstoyan scope," that the books are "an astonishing overview of the whole war"? Was Burgess demonstrating the absence of a "valid standard" when he wrote that "the book I've done covers something of Nazi Germany but it lacks your metaphysics"? And when Burgess tells Wouk that "your work makes me ask so many questions that it evidently belongs to the big philosophical tradition"—is not Burgess judging by a "valid standard"?

What has escaped the notice of the professional critics is that Wouk's war novels—when he began the first he was fifty and when he finished the second he was sixty-three—have made bestsellerdom without formulaic gobs of eroticism, perversion, hallucinatory onanism, incest, lesbianism, necrophilia, and a generalized scatology. A unique achievement these days. It would seem that there is an American and even a world readership which still yearns for the traditional novel, a story full of invention, coincidences, surprises, suspense, ideas, and a moral. And when this readership finds such an artist it stays with him without regard for what their betters tell them and, surprisingly, not minding "its burdensome thousand-page bulk." Such a sustained success without national television book-promotion tours and idiotic interviews with illiterates pretending to be reporters is not too common in America. And that, too, is a kind of achievement—to let a book speak for itself, for its own value, without the vulgar, exploitative marketing in which the author becomes shill to the publisher. This is not for Wouk who once said: "In my selection of themes, stories, and characters, I speak for conserving what I value best in civilization, for I think a bright future will be built on these things when the storm has passed if we can manage to preserve enough of what was and remains good."[4]

In a famous essay John Ruskin said that books are divisible into two classes—"the books of the hour and the books of all time." Ruskin called the latter "true books," written "not to multiply the voice merely, not to carry it merely, but to perpetuate it." The author of a "true book," writes Ruskin, is saying:

> "This is the best of me; for the rest, I ate, and drank, and slept, loved, and hated, like another; my life was as the vapour, and is not; but this I saw and knew: this, if anything of mine, is worth your memory." That is his "writing"; it is, in his small human way, and with whatever degree of true inspiration is in him, his inscription, or scripture. That is a "Book."[5]

That is Herman Wouk.

NOTES

1. Interview in *Book World* (26 December 1971):14. Newspaper or magazine interviews with Wouk are quite rare. He avoids radio and television appearances as well. He might find it easy to agree with Simone de Beauvoir, once a target of an importunate press, who said she understood

that the reporters were only doing their job: "Agreed; I have nothing against them; some of my best friends are journalists," she said. "I just don't like the newspapers they work for. Furthermore, with the best will in the world, or the worst, publicity disfigures those who fall into its hands. In my view, the relation a writer entertains with the truth makes it impossible for him to acquiesce to such treatment; it is quite enough that it should be inflicted upon one." *Times Literary Supplement* (28 August 1981):978.

2. Christopher Lehmann-Haupt, "Books of the Times," *New York Times* (6 November 1978).
3. Pearl K. Bell, "Good-Bad and Bad-Bad," *Commentary* (December 1978):70-72.
4. Letter to author from Wouk (8 August 1980). For a fuller and more organized exposition see "You, Me, and the Novel," *Saturday Review* (29 June 1974):8-13. The essay was adapted by Wouk from an extemporaneous talk at The Aspen Institute, where in 1973 he was scholar-in-residence.
5. John Ruskin, "Of King's Treasuries," in *Sesame And Lillies* (London: Allen, 1908):11, 12, 14.

Bibliography

PRIMARY SOURCES: HERMAN WOUK

Novels

Aurora Dawn: Or the True History of Andrew Reale, Containing a Faithful Account of the Great Riot, Together with the Complete Texts of Michael Wilde's Oration and Father Stanfield's Sermon. New York: Simon & Schuster, 1947.
Slattery's Hurricane. A screen treatment for Paramount Pictures, 1948. New York: Pocket Books, 1956.
The Caine Mutiny. New York: Doubleday, 1951.
The City Boy. New York: Doubleday, 1952.
Marjorie Morningstar. New York: Doubleday, 1955.
The "Lomokome" Papers. In *Collier's,* 1956. New York: Pocket Books, 1968.
Youngblood Hawke. New York: Doubleday, 1962.
Don't Stop the Carnival. New York: Doubleday, 1965.
The Winds of War. Boston: Little, Brown, 1971.
War and Remembrance. Boston: Little, Brown, 1978.

Essays

This Is My God. Garden City, N.Y.: Doubleday, 1959. "Introduction" to *Self-Portrait of a Hero: The Letters of Jonathan Netanyahu.* New York: Random House, 1980.

Plays

The Traitor. New York: Samuel French, 1949.
The Caine Mutiny Court-Martial. New York: Doubleday, 1954.
Nature's Way. Garden City, N.Y.: Doubleday, 1958.

Others

Letters, notebooks, and interviews in uncatalogued Wouk Collection, Butler Library, Columbia University, New York, N.Y.

SECONDARY SOURCES

Works of Criticism

Edmund Fuller, *Man in Modern Fiction* (New York: Random House, 1958). Modern fiction seen as exemplifying various theories as to the nature of man. A discussion of *The Caine Mutiny* deals not only with the novel but also with the general tenor of critical response to the novel.

Maxwell Geismar, *American Moderns from Rebellion to Conformity* (New York: Hill & Wang, 1958). A collection of critical essays and reviews from the 1940s and 1950s. Contains Geismar's review of *Marjorie Morningstar* for the *New York Times* (4 September 1955) and an essay from the *Nation* (5 November 1955) on the *Time* cover story (5 September 1955) about Wouk.

Allen Guttman, *The Jewish Writer in America: Assimilation and the Crisis in Identity* (New York: Oxford University Press, 1971). Analysis of *The Caine Mutiny* and *Marjorie Morningstar* in the context of an examination of Jewish authors in America.

James D. Hart, *The Popular Book: A History of America's Literary Taste* (New York: Oxford University Press, 1950). A comprehensive and scholarly study of popular fiction in America.

Stanley Edgar Hyman, *Standards: A Chronicle of Books for Our Time* (New York: Horizon, 1966). Among the most trenchant and hostile of Wouk's critics, particularly of *Youngblood Hawke*.

Peter G. Jones, *War and the Novelist: Appraising the American War Novel* (Ann Arbor: University of Michigan Press, 1976). *The Caine Mutiny* is discussed in relation to other war novels dealing with the problems of command.

Leslie Fiedler, *Love and Death in the American Novel* (New York: Criterion, 1960). Provocative, erudite, and highly idiosyncratic discussions of American novels, *Marjorie Morningstar* among them.

W.J. Stuckey, *The Pulitzer Prize Novels: A Critical Backward Look* (Norman: University of Oklahoma Press, 1966). A book which sets out to assess the overall quality of the Pulitzer Prize-winning novels, including *The Caine Mutiny*.

Albert Van Nostrand, *The Denatured Novel* (Indianapolis, Ind.: Bobbs-Merrill, 1956). Witty and incisive account of the development of the popular novel, containing an assessment of *The Caine Mutiny*.

Joseph J. Waldemeir, *American Novelists of the Second World War* (The Hague: Mouton, 1969). Contains an assessment of *The Caine Mutiny* from the vantage of the late 1960s.

William H. Whyte, *The Organization Man* (New York: Doubleday-Anchor, 1956). Primarily a work of sociology or cultural anthropology. The author discusses the conclusion of *The Caine Mutiny* as part of the general analysis of tensions between the individual and organizations in the twentieth century.

W.T. Witham, *The Adolescent in the American Novel, 1920-1960* (New York: Ungar, 1964). Discusses *The City Boy* and *Marjorie Morningstar*.

Reviews, Essays

P.K. Bell, *Commentary* 66 (December 1978):70-72.
Paul Fussell, *New Republic* 179 (14 October 1978):32-33.
B. Kalb, *Saturday Review of Literature* 38 (3 September 1955):9.
N. Podhoretz, "Jew as Bourgeois," *Commentary* 21 (February 1956):186-88.
A. Schlesinger, Jr., "Time and the Intellectuals," *New Republic* 135 (16 July 1956):15-17.
"Wouk Mutiny," *Time* 66 (5 September 1955):48-50 (cover story).

Times Literary Supplement (7 October 1955):594; (8 July 1965):573.

H. Swados, "Popular Taste and the Caine Mutiny," *Partisan Review* (March-April 1953).

Granville Hicks, "The Novel Isn't Dying," *New Leader* (10 December 1951).

Joseph Cohen, "Wouk's Morningstar and Hemingway's Sun," *South Atlantic Quarterly* 58 (Spring 1959):213-24.

Irwin Ross, six article series with Wouk letter, *New York Post* (beginning 22 January 1956).

H. Colby, Biographical sketch, *Wilson Library Bulletin* 26 (March 1952).

Michael Mandelbaum, "The Political Lessons of Two World War II Novels: A Review Essay," *Political Science Quarterly* 94 (Fall 1979):515-22.

Index